D0762370

Maintaining Diversity in Higher Education

Robert Birnbaum

assisted by

Estela Mara Bensimon

Maintaining Diversity in Higher Education

Jossey-Bass Publishers
San Francisco • Washington • London • 1983

MAINTAINING DIVERSITY IN HIGHER EDUCATION
by Robert Birnbaum

433 California Street
San Francisco, California 94104
&
Jossey-Bass Limited
28 Banner Street
London EC1Y 8QE

Figure 1 from *Contingency Views of Organization and Management* by Fremont E. Kast and James E. Rosenzweig. © 1973, Science Research Associates, Inc. Reprinted by permission of the publisher.

Library of Congress Cataloging in Publication Data

Birnbaum, Robert.
Maintaining diversity in higher education.

Bibliography: p. 188
Includes index.
1. Universities and colleges—United States—Evaluation. 2. Educational surveys—United States. 3. Education, Higher—United States—Aims and objectives.
I. Title.
LB2331.63.B57 1983 378.73 83-48156
ISBN 0-87589-574-3

Manufactured in the United States of America

The paper in this book meets the guidelines for permanence and durability of the Committee on Production Guidelines for Book Longevity of the Council on Library Resources.

JACKET DESIGN BY WILLI BAUM

FIRST EDITION

Code 8321

The Jossey-Bass
Higher Education Series

Preface

A major question for biologists is "Why are there so many different kinds of animals?" Social scientists ask a parallel question for the same reasons: "Why are there so many different kinds of organizations?" (Hannan and Freeman, 1977, p. 956).

In higher education we too can point to the varied and diverse forms of institutions populating the academic landscape and inquire "Why are there so many different kinds of colleges and universities?" We do not usually ask the question in quite this way. Rather, we assert that it is essential to have different kinds of institutions, and we express concern when the survival of particular kinds of institutions appears to be threatened. Diversity is assumed to be good. Indeed, it would probably not be unfair to identify institutional diversity as one of the major ideological pillars of American higher education. As is true with other major educational concepts with strong ethical and policy components, such as "access" or "quality," the idea of diversity can provoke debate even while—or perhaps because—it eludes common and accepted definition. Why is diversity important? How can it be measured? Is it increasing or decreasing? What public policies can enhance or restrict it?

This book proposes some answers to these questions by empirically analyzing changes in the population of higher education institutions over the twenty-year period between 1960 and 1980. It differs from previous examinations of diversity in higher education in that it emphasizes the effects of the environment on changes in institutional form, and it views colleges and universities as evolving parts of a system whose components change as a consequence of natural selection. These evolutionary processes create a diversity of organizational forms that reflect the diversity of the environments in which they developed (Hawley, 1968; Hannan and Freeman, 1977). Why are there so many different kinds of colleges and universities? Because the American social system provides so many different "niches" for them to fill. Why is diversity important? Because it ensures a system of higher education that is at once stable and responsive to the demands of its social environments.

Natural selection, of course, is a concept developed in population ecology to account for the evolution of biological species. Over the past ten years it has been proposed as a useful perspective for examining changes in populations of organizations as well. In order for the evolution of organizational populations to be studied through the three stages of the natural selection process—variation, selection, and retention—several requirements must be met. One of these requirements is that there must be a clear, unequivocal way of classifying organizations into categories equivalent to species in biology. Existing institutional typologies are unsatisfactory for this purpose (see, for example, typologies in Carnegie Commission, 1973a; Baldridge and others, 1978; Carnegie Council, 1976; Makowski and Wulfsberg, 1980); their categories are too few in number and too broad in composition, and they emphasize the identification of institutional commonalities rather than differences. This book suggests a new way of differentiating institutions that, at the same time, permits clustering colleges and universities according to important structural and program similarities. The resulting clusters serve as "institutional species" for the purposes of measuring and analyzing diversity.

The methodology employed in this book is simple. First, the types of institutions existing in 1960 in eight selected states are identified and their distribution in the population determined. The same analysis is then repeated for every institution existing in 1980. For each distribution, a "diversity index" is then calculated, providing a quantitative indicator that permits measurement of changes in the level of diversity during the twenty-year period.

The eight states were chosen on the basis of size, geography, and state coordinating system. They include within them approximately 30 percent of all colleges and universities in the country; although not randomly selected, they are in many ways similar to the total national population of institutions of higher education. The findings reported in this study can thus be used to understand changes in diversity on a national level.

The index can be used to study changes in diversity over time or to assess the comparative level of diversity in two geographic locations. It can also be used by researchers as a dependent variable (for example, to determine whether state support of private higher education is related to the level of institutional diversity) or as an independent variable (for example, to assess whether minority student enrollment is likely to be higher in states with greater institutional diversity). It should be a new and useful tool for policy analysis.

Chapter One discusses the importance of diversity in American higher education, beginning with the familiar arguments concerning its benefits in meeting complex and varying student needs as well as in responding to other social and political demands. The chapter then presents a new perspective on the role of diversity in an open system characterized by responsiveness to the environment. Particular emphasis is given to the essential function of diversity in providing the variability that is a precondition for natural selection and organizational evolution.

Because treatments in the past have tended to offer relatively narrow definitions of diversity, Chapter Two describes a number of different ways of looking at the phenomenon. Seven approaches to institutional diversity are presented and discussed, each of which is doubtless valid for some purpose. But the lack of a commonly accepted definition has led different scholars to base their analyses on completely different sets and combinations of variables. For this reason, while there is universal agreement on the desirability of maintaining diversity in higher education, there is considerable disagreement on the present level of diversity in the system and on whether that level is increasing or decreasing. The various positions on these issues are reviewed in Chapter Three, and a new analysis is offered based on open-systems theory. That perspective suggests that since the environment within which colleges and universities exist has become more uniform in recent decades, institutional diversity has likely been correspondingly reduced.

The methodology of the study is discussed in Chapter Four, including the basis for selection of the eight states and of the component variables that together are used to differentiate between institutional "types." The data collected for the study are then analyzed in two ways. In Chapter Five, the characteristics of the sample of institutions in 1960 and in 1980 are presented. Comparisons show not only how the population of institutions differed during the two periods but also the extent to which such differences reflected the development of new institutions, the demise or merging of old ones, and the transformation of those that existed over the entire twenty-year period. Chapter Six then describes how variables were combined so that institutions could be clustered into "types" analogous to species in biology. Several methods of creating a diversity index are proposed and applied, first to the total sample and then state by state. A preferred index is selected and used to compare the distribution of species and their concentrations during 1960 and during 1980 and to determine to what extent diversity in the system has changed. The results indicate that while American higher education is still diverse, the level of diversity has decreased over the past twenty years.

Chapter Seven considers the implications of the study for

public policy. Particular attention is given to potential directions and alternatives made visible by the natural selection model. Because of the complex and interdependent relationship between the environment and a population of institutions, many of the policy recommendations are counterintuitive and provocative. The chapter argues, among other things, that viability of the higher education system requires that some institutions fail, that "waste" is an essential element in system effectiveness, that attempts to control "quality" may create systemic weakness, and that system diversity is likely to decrease as planning for diversity increases. The chapter suggests effective strategies for survival that institutions in different environments may employ; it also offers guidance to state systems whose present policies may constrain the processes of natural selection.

The book does not propose that there is a single or even a "best" definition of diversity—the concept itself is too diverse for that. But it does offer a new way of looking at the issue that is analytic and embedded in a coherent conceptual framework. This approach should be of interest to college and university administrators, officers of multicampus systems and state coordinating boards, professional organizations, political groups and others concerned with the development of public policy, and, of course, students of higher education and of organizations.

Acknowledgments

I would like to recognize several important sources of financial, administrative, and intellectual support in completing this study. I am grateful to the National Institute of Education for funding this work through a research grant and to Robert J. (Rocky) Schwarz and his colleagues at the Teachers College Word Processing Center for their prompt and accurate work through several drafts and innumerable changes. I also wish to thank Richard E. Anderson and Wagner Thielens of Teachers College, Raymond F. Zammuto of the National Center for Higher Education Management Systems, John Wirt of the National Institute of Education, and JB Lon Hefferlin of the California Postsecondary Education Commission for their careful reading, thoughtful support, and constructive criticisms at various points in the preparation of the manuscript. Their collegial helpfulness, of course, by no means implies their endorsement of the ideas presented here.

Finally, I wish to acknowledge the contributions of Estela Mara Bensimon who, prior to receiving the doctoral degree from the Department of Higher and Adult Education at Teachers College, was the research assistant for this study. She was responsible for the collection, coding, and computer analysis of the data reported here, as well as for drafting portions of several chapters. In addition to providing professional research support of the highest caliber, her critical comments and original suggestions at many points during the research and writing significantly strengthened the final study.

New York, New York Robert Birnbaum
July 1983

Contents

The Author

Robert Birnbaum is professor of higher education at Teachers College, Columbia University. He received the B.A. degree in psychology from the University of Rochester (1958) and the M.A. degree (1964) and Ed.D. degree (1967) in higher education from Teachers College.

Prior to his faculty appointment, Birnbaum held administrative positions in a number of different academic settings, and has served as vice-chancellor of the City University of New York, vice-chancellor of the New Jersey Department of Higher Education, and chancellor of the University of Wisconsin–Oshkosh.

His research has appeared in the *Journal of Higher Education, Review of Higher Education, Educational Record, Journal of Educational Research,* and other major scholarly and professional journals. Recent publications include *Creative Academic Bargaining: Managing Conflict in the Unionized College and*

University (1980) and the chapter entitled "Higher Education" in the fifth edition of the *Encyclopedia of Educational Research* (1982). His present research interests focus on the application of concepts of organization behavior and applied behavioral science to improve both the theory and the practice of academic bargaining, governance, and college and university administration.

Maintaining Diversity in Higher Education

1

Value of Different Kinds of Colleges

Diversity is widely believed to be an essential characteristic of American higher education, one that in many ways differentiates postsecondary institutions in this country from those of other nations (Clark and Youn, 1976). Diversity has been identified as one of the basic reasons for higher education's high level of performance in this country (Carnegie Commission, 1973b; Carnegie Foundation, 1975; Sloan Commission, 1980) and an essential element in ensuring the system's responsiveness to societal needs (Ben-David, 1972; Trow, 1979).

Stadtman (1980) compiled a representative listing of the benefits of diversity. He indicated that institutional diversity

- increases the range of choices available to learners
- makes higher education available to virtually everyone, despite differences among individuals
- matches education to the needs, goals, learning styles, speed, and ability of individual students
- enables institutions to select their own missions and confine their activities to those which are consistent with their location, resources, levels of instruction, and clienteles

- responds to the pressures of a society that is itself characterized by great complexity and diversity
- becomes a precondition of college and university freedom and autonomy because the greater the differences are among institutions, the more difficult it is for a central authority to convert them into instruments of indoctrination rather than of education [pp. 98-99].

This chapter considers the importance of institutional diversity in somewhat greater detail. For convenience, the justifications for diversity are grouped under three categories. First are the arguments for diversity based upon *institutional* grounds related to such educational matters as curriculum development and student needs. The second category is the *societal* arguments for diversity, which view higher education as fulfilling political, social, and economic functions in addition to their stated educational purposes. The third grouping includes issues that relate diversity to *systemic* needs—those factors that affect the higher education system's ability as a whole to remain stable, even as it evolves in response to environmental changes.

These categories present three different perspectives on diversity: the relationships of institutions to clienteles, to other social systems, and to themselves. Note that these three perspectives are interconnected, so arguments made from one of them could, in many cases, be made for another. For this reason, the boundaries between the perspectives are not quite clear and the placement of arguments in one or another grouping may be arbitrary to some extent.

In the past, the greatest attention by far has been paid to diversity based upon institutional grounds, with less emphasis upon societal factors and little at all upon the functions of system change and stability. Thus, this chapter focuses upon the neglected third aspect, beginning, however, with relatively brief discussions of the other two.

Institutional Arguments for Diversity

Meeting Students' Needs. Arguments in support of institutional diversity based upon students' needs are themselves diverse. Historically, the most important one has been the desire for a religious environment compatible with the teachings of one's own church, a motivation that influenced the founding of eight of the nine original colonial colleges and hundreds of institutions prior to the Civil War. Although perhaps of less importance today, it is still true that many students and their parents seek an institution in which a particular set of religious values accompanies (or in some cases permeates) the teaching of traditional academic subjects.

For most students, however, other factors are seen as more critical. Students with varying histories of academic achievement have access to institutions whose performance expectations also vary, thus affording each student the opportunity to compete with others of similar background. This makes it possible for *A* as well as *C* or *D* high school students to find environments in which chances for success are realistic.

Some students prefer the intimate atmosphere and possibility for personal attention that a small campus offers; others find such an environment stultifying and prefer the more cosmopolitan climate and wider range of programs and student subcultures available in large institutions.

Students' needs are also reflected in the diverse orientations of many institutions' programs, which range from those with unique support services for students with learning disabilities, physical handicaps, or the need for remedial or developmental work to those with special curriculum emphases. Cross (1976) suggested that institutions recognize the diverse interests of "new learners" by expanding definitions of excellence so that students might earn degrees not only by exhibiting their mastery of ideas but, alternatively, by demonstrating proficiency in either working with physical things or with people. To some extent, the diversity of institutions today makes it possible for students to select schools and programs in which proficiency in one of these three areas will be the major criterion by which they will be judged (or at least will be the major outcome of their experience).

Students' needs may also be met through the characteristics of the other students attending the same institution. Opportunities to attend institutions enrolling only men or only women may benefit those students for whom not having to compete with the opposite sex is important (Riesman, 1975; Astin, 1977). Historically, black colleges offer black students an alternative to the environments of predominantly white colleges and universities as well as a chance to work with faculty who understand the black experience, and they give white students an opportunity to experience being in a minority role (Thompson, 1978). Community-based institutions reflect and transmit the culture of the communities in which they are located and may give particular attention to the distinct and possibly atypical learning needs of the student body (Smith and Bernstein, 1979).

The range of interests to which institutions must respond is enormous, as Breneman and Finn (1978) pointed out: "Some students thrive, for instance, in large universities, others in small colleges; some like competitive settings, others prefer nurturing environments; some want to live away from home, others must commute; some desire technical and vocational preparation, others favor the liberal arts; some want a secure, in loco parentis institution that inculcates values and tells them what to study, others want one offering a vast smorgasbord of electives; some seek schools with high academic standards giving entry to post-secondary study, while others prefer to test the water in an open admissions institution; and there are always those who want schools with a tradition of serving a particular race, sex, or denomination" (p. 416).

No single kind of institution, regardless of its internal diversity, and no structured educational system based upon the Continental model (Clark and Youn, 1976) could begin to reflect the degree to which a number of American colleges and universities have developed in response to the unique needs and interests of certain communities of students. Even with this differentiation, however, the institutional system has been criticized, not for being too diverse, but for not being diverse enough to reflect fully students' differing backgrounds, learning styles, and individual interests (Newman, 1971).

In meeting students' differing needs, a diverse system serves not only the interests of individuals but the interests of the public. New Jersey, which exports more students than any state in the union, discovered that a majority of students leaving the state attend institutions with special characteristics not represented in the array of New Jersey institutions. The state chancellor of higher education has been quoted as saying that "for all practical purposes, unless we open new institutions, we would expect these students to continue to leave the state" (Feldman, 1981).

Insufficient diversity in New Jersey is likely to exacerbate projected enrollment declines, making management of the state higher education system even more difficult over the next decade than it might otherwise be. In addition, there are fiscal costs to the diversity-related "brain drain"; those who leave the state for their higher education often do not return, but if the migrating students stayed in the state, they would be expected to return at least $34 million each year to the state's economy.

Increasing Institutional Effectiveness. Institutions of higher education are called upon to perform many important functions for society. In many cases, the institutional structures, personnel, resources, and traditions that are essential preconditions for effectively performing one of these functions (transmission of culture through the liberal arts, for example) are quite different from those required for successfully performing another and equally important function (basic biomedical research, for example). Evidence suggests that effective achievement of certain goals in a single college or university requires that less attention be given to others (Cameron, 1978); in other words, the effectiveness of the system increases as institutions differentiate and place primary attention upon specific missions and goals.

Understanding the relationship between differentiation and institutional effectiveness, the Carnegie Commission (1973b) noted that certain functions may not fit together well on a single campus and suggested that "the search for excellence can be aided by specialization which allows not only a concentration of attention and effort, but also a higher status for some endeavors than they would have if they were subordinated to others in the same institution" (p. 72). The commission recommended that institutions reconsider their various functions and activities and avoid and eliminate noncomplementary functions.

The fact that, among other achievements, our higher education system has managed both to provide a level of access not seen in any other nation and to become internationally preeminent in scientific research has, in large measure, been made possible by the existence of a diverse system that includes institutions able to specialize in each area. If all institutions had had the same goals, structures, technologies, and constituencies, most likely the system as a whole could not have excelled in as many areas of endeavor.

Providing Models. Because of the problematic technology and ambiguous goals of most institutions of higher education, it is exceptionally difficult to predict accurately the consequences of new programs or procedures or to determine in advance the effectiveness of alternative ways of responding to new forces in the environment. If all institutions were the same, they would have little to guide decisions, other than their own limited rationality or conformity to choices made by others. Having little precedence to guide their decisions, they would be as likely to err as to be correct; indeed, they would be *more* likely to err, since in institutions, as in nature, most changes are not for the good.

In a diverse system, however, institutions and subsystems of institutions have a rich source of data not available in those that are centrally planned and coordinated—the various programs and experiences of a large number of institutions that have experimented and responded in diverse ways and that can therefore serve as models. In a diverse system, models constitute naturalistic experiments that can be examined by other institutions. From the models, the institutions can assess with a greater degree of assurance the viability of certain approaches, the probable outcomes of specific decisions, and the effects of new structures or orientations, without necessarily having to implement the same changes themselves. These models are usually thought of as reflecting innovations related to good practice, but in many ways they are even more effective in providing examples of things to avoid. They may serve as exemplars whose programs or new directions might be adapted partly or entirely by other institutions, or they may influence the entire system indirectly but perhaps more powerfully by successfully challenging the conventional wisdom, thereby changing the perception of others even if they adopt none of its specific characteristics. The models may have preserved unique ways of doing things that had little relevance to the system when they were initiated but now have a new relevance, or they may act as a laboratory for experiments that may, in ways not currently known, be useful for future unforeseen problems.

For example, private institutions offer as a model the effects of having extraordinary flexibility in developing new programs (El-Khawas, 1976), and they have had experiences dealing with budget constraints and organizational renewal problems that are particularly important to many institutions in today's political and economic environment (Jonsen, 1978). Proprietary institutions, once scorned for their occupational orientations, marketing approach, and need to operate frugally to make a profit, may now have a knowledge of "lean models" that is of interest and value to other kinds of postsecondary institutions (Trivett, 1974).

Academic change and innovation in this country have been affected by both the significant external forces to which institutions have been subjected and the creative responses to these pressures by a few institutions that have served as models for others in the system. Grant and Riesman (1978) wrote that "Just as the experimental colleges which were fugitive on many campuses led faculty to conclude that they would not be outoptioned by the pedagogic left, so the small pioneers like New College in Sarasota, Hampshire, and, in the public domain, Santa Cruz, had an influence out of all proportion to their numbers. In the past, academic reforms seem to have begun either in the kinds of offbeat, mostly private colleges . . . or in the major research-oriented universities, and to have spread as graduates of these institutions went to teach in places beyond the vanguard orbits. Today, the chains of influence are less hierarchical" (p. 380).

Diverse institutions' ability to establish individually new programs or policies significantly lowers the risk of change for the entire system. If the changes appear viable, other institutions may seek to adapt portions of them for their own use. If the changes turn out to have negative consequences, other institutions have been spared the ordeal of learning through experience. Diversity thus permits low-risk experimentation (from a system perspective), since failure is isolated to single institutions. Antioch's experiences with satellite campuses and the consequences of Parsons College's vigorously entrepreneurial orientation were as useful to other institutions by their failure as they would have been had they been successful. Although such experimentation can occur in either the public or private sector, Riesman pointed out that they are more likely to occur in private institutions "which remain small (and recruit a distinctive constituency) by choice, and which do not need to fear direct legislative or other political reprisal if the experiment turns sour" (Breneman and Finn, 1978, p. 422). At the same time, certain experiments can take place *only* in the public sector. The experience of City University of New York, for example, provided models of what to do (and what not to do) in implementing policies of open admissions in an urban setting.

New models developed at one institution can be disseminated to others in many traditional ways: through reports in professional journals and books and by formal and informal communications between educators at professional and scholarly meetings. Perhaps as important, although seldom commented upon or studied, is the role of personnel mobility. Faculty and administrators who move from one college to another may bring with them new ideas that can influence their new institution. Although no data are available, it is possible that such mobility (at least in the past) has been higher among persons who have worked at innovative institutions and have been "burned out" and exhausted by the efforts of innovation. An indication that "veteran" faculty at such innovative institutions as Monteith and Oakland later made major contributions to the undergraduate curricula at many other campuses (Riesman, Gusfield, and Gamson, 1970) suggests the apparent paradox that innovative institutions can serve as latent models even to other institutions that do not know of them!

Protecting Institutional Autonomy and Academic Freedom. Academic freedom is academe's most cherished value. The "free search for truth and its free exposition" is critical because it provides the rationale for the structures and processes of colleges and universities in this country today. More than that, however, academic freedom is a reflection of societal values that see institutions of higher education as conducted for the common good and freedom in teaching and research as essential to achieving that common good. The American Association of University Professors' *1940 Statement of Principles on Academic Freedom and Tenure* delineates this relationship: "Freedom in research is fundamental to the advancement of truth. Academic freedom in its teaching aspect is fundamental for the protection of the rights of the teacher in teaching and of the student in freedom in learning. . . . Freedom . . . [is] indispensable to the success of an institution in fulfilling its obligations to its students and to society" (1977, p. 2).

The relationship between academic freedom and institutional diversity, while perhaps indirect, is quite strong. Institutions of varying sizes, control, or constituency have been involved in abuses of academic freedom, so it is not possible to single out one sector as being the untainted guardian of the faith. Yet there is concern that, despite the enviable records in the twentieth century of such public institutions of international stature as the Universities of Wisconsin, Michigan, or Minnesota, the ultimate protection of the principles of academic freedom rests upon the existence of institutions not dependent for their survival upon an elected legislature responsive to sudden changes in the public mood. As Riesman (1975) put it, "Academic freedom has not invariably been better protected by the trustees of private institutions, but the fear of offending a state legislator or governor is infinitely greater in the public institutions than the fear of offending a particular wealthy donor in the major private institutions, especially in those which have developed strong alumni loyalty and a kind of patrician restraint among donors" (p. 471).

But it is not only the freedom from political interference that marks the potential academic freedom issues in higher education; also at stake are the values likely to be given prominence by institutions supported by public or private sources. As

Breneman and Finn (1978) suggested, "Pluralistic governance and independence are intrinsically important to untrammeled inquiry, scholarly excellence, and educational diversity. With the best will in the world, the fifty state governments are unlikely to emphasize adequately such subtle, vulnerable, and inherently 'private' values" (p. 423).

Threats to academic freedom of course come not only from public agencies whose perceived interests at any given moment might suggest the desirability of subordinating academic freedom to some "higher" good. Other institutions, or categories of institutions both public and private, from time to time may purposefully or inadvertently pursue goals in response to religious orthodoxy, fiscal survival, popular mood of constituencies on or off campus, or a lack of thoughtful attention to the potential consequences of actions taken in the name of accountability or some other important administrative objective. In a diverse system, the crosscutting pressures upon institutions are so varied that there is never a situation in which all institutions —or even a majority—face the same threats to academic freedom. Diversity thus provides both a systemic capacity to identify such threats as they are manifested in other institutions and a countervailing force to aberrant behaviors by calling attention to them.

Societal Arguments for Diversity

From an institutional perspective, the purpose of a college or university, or a system of such institutions, is primarily educational, and institutions' teaching, research, and service missions can be examined, as they were in the previous section, to determine the influence of diversity. Although this view can be revealing, it is incomplete because higher education is intimately connected to, and therefore interacts with, other societal systems. Without denying the primary importance of their educational purposes, clearly higher educational institutions also serve political, economic, and social functions, and they have done so since the founding of the first colleges in this country. Regarding the reasons for establishing the colonial colleges, Rudolph (1962) wrote: "A college develops a sense of unity where, in a society created from many of the nations of Europe, there might otherwise be aimlessness and uncontrolled diversity. A college advances learning; it combats ignorance and barbarism. A college is a support of the state; it is an instructor in loyalty, in citizenship, in the dictates of conscience and faith. A college is useful; it helps men to learn the things they must know in order to manage the temporal affairs of the world; it trains a legion of teachers. All these things a college was. All these purposes a college served" (p. 13).

Societal purposes are served not only by academic institutions but by their diversity. This section discusses several such purposes.

Providing for Social Mobility. Although there is compelling evidence that rates of social mobility in this country have not increased with increased opportunities for higher education (Jencks and Riesman, 1977), it is generally accepted as a matter of faith that a major purpose of our system of colleges and universities is to provide avenues for mobility. Opportunities to move between social classes over a generation prevent the formation of rigid castes that would make the management of conflict extremely difficult in a pluralistic society. If mobility rates have not in fact increased, that they have remained stable during a period of increased demands for professional and technical competence is probably due to the activities of colleges and universities.

Institutional diversity serves these mobility interests by offering a number of different modes of entry into the academic system. Students who cannot gain admission to a selective liberal arts college can start on the road toward the baccalaureate as well as advanced professional and academic degrees by attending the local community college, which is open to all high school graduates (and in some areas, to nongraduates over a certain age). Multiple routes of access, coupled with the screening functions of the institutions themselves, have led to what Ben-David (1972) referred to as an integrated system. "There are practically no blind alleys in it. One can always transfer from one level to another, and it is easy to transfer from one institution to another, especially between degrees. In practice, these possibilities are limited by the evaluation of the qualities of different colleges, but there are, nevertheless, cases of transfer from practically any type of accredited institution to any other type" (p. 7).

The diversity of institutions, coupled with the integration of the system, means that, unlike in many other countries, there are no errors of student academic judgment that cannot be rectified at some point, no early and final screening that eliminates all but a select few from future consideration for advanced study, and little basis for a student to claim that the higher educational system does not offer opportunities for success. Riesman (1975) pointed out that this consequence of diversity has not been sufficiently recognized. "It means that the United States is a country of second chances and even third chances. Poorly guided, perhaps poorly motivated, perhaps lacking a sufficient horizon on one's own interests and on the world, a young person may make a start in a college of low academic and intellectual caliber and then transfer as, for example, is actually impossible in the United Kingdom, to a college of higher quality" (p. 481).

Diversity and systemic integration provide not only for upward mobility but for honorable downward mobility. Students with aspirations inappropriate to their ability can leave an institution in which they are not competitive and enter another setting in which the other students' achievements more nearly match their own. This intrasystem mobility serves somewhat the same "cooling out" function as the intrainstitutional mobility of students between community colleges' transfer and career programs. In both cases, the mobility makes student failure at one level less traumatic because of the availability of opportunities at less demanding levels.

Serving the Political Needs of Interest Groups. The rapid growth in the number of institutions during the early and mid-nineteenth century generally was due more to the desire of various interest groups for institutions that would meet their own unique needs than to the pressures of increased interest in college-going. In many cases, the educational rationale for such institutions was the perpetuation of a culture and the protection of the identity of one or another religious, ethnic, geographical, or socioeconomic subgroup. "The pervasive sectarianism of American religious life remained after 1770, as before that date, the most common source of the impulse to found a new college. Each sect wished to train its own ministers, hold the loyalty of its young people, and convert outsiders; it was plausible to imagine that an institution of higher education would serve all those purposes . . ." (Handlin and Handlin, 1970, p. 25).

But often, behind these avowed educational purposes were strong political motivations. Sponsoring a college not only helped perpetuate a distinct subculture, it gave it "legitimacy in the larger society" (Jencks and Riesman, 1977, p. 3). Today, the relative esteem in which colleges and universities are held establishes an aura of respectability around any group that is able to found an academic institution. This partly accounts for the rapid development of fundamentalist institutions such as Bob Jones University and Liberty Baptist College, or the importance that the National Unification Church, for example, attaches to their attempt to gain approval in New York State for a degree-granting seminary. There are many ways groups with norms and aspirations inconsistent with the dominant culture can attempt to establish visibility and legitimacy; certainly the opportunity to create an institution called a college is one of the more peaceful and constructive ways.

Visibility and legitimacy, as well as economic advantage, also have played major roles in the establishment of colleges based upon regional interests. In the nineteenth century, communities vied with each other over the location of colleges that, it was thought, would prove attractive to potential residents. "When public support of higher education developed, rival communities fought bitter battles to secure projected new institutions. . . . Often these were distributed . . . as political plums to satisfy the demands of local interest groups" (Brubacher and Rudy, 1976, p. 60).

Today, interest in locating colleges probably centers more upon the schools' attractiveness to industry than increasing the size of the local population, but the continued relationship between civic pride and college location, even in the absence of economic benefit, should not be minimized. Today, as in the past, colleges are as likely to be started for political as for educational reasons. For example, the formation of a Ramapo College in northern New Jersey was very much dependent upon a local politician's ability to get his way in having a Stockton State College in the pine barrens of southern New Jersey approved (Grant and Riesman, 1978).

These political purposes of higher education can be met best by a diverse system, not only because it ensures that the needs of different groups for identity and legitimation can be met, but because it does so while protecting the stability of the system itself. The maintenance of diversity serves much the same purpose within a system that Eliot's development of the elective system at Harvard in the mid-nineteenth century did within an institution. As debates concerning matters such as the proper role of religious education or the acceptability of new areas of study and teaching methodology ensued during a time of great social change in American life, Eliot chose the elective system as a way of silencing the debate without requiring that any faction lose it. As Ben-David (1972) observed, "Attempts to commit institutions to a given philosophy would have given rise to acrimonious debates and would have split the college community into warring factions" (p. 56). With the development of the elective system, these choices could be made by individuals rather than by institutions, and "a major educational reform was achieved without the necessity of making institutional decisions about educational values" (p. 57).

In the same way, on a systemic level, fundamental religious groups interested in developing college opportunities for their children away from the environmental pressures of more liberal institutions (Riesman, 1975) are able to do so through the expediency of founding new institutions, without requiring a major public debate on the purposes and ideologies of existing institutions. In a less diverse system, the needs of such groups would be likely to either remain unaddressed or provoke changes in the system as a whole, which would cause unusual disruption and internal debate. As Clark (1976) pointed out, in a unitary system, "any important change in one part or another becomes a national issue requiring debate and enactment at the center and implementation across the system" (p. 33).

Permitting Both Elite and Mass Higher Education. If quality and access can be considered two of the major ideological commitments of the American system of higher education, the development of institutions serving an elite student body, as well as those providing opportunities for serving the need of mass higher education, provides the operational means by which these two apparently conflicting values can be accommodated within a single system. This in turn requires a commitment to the concept of institutional diversity, thus permitting what Clark (1981) called the capacity to face simultaneously in different directions.

The exceptional difficulty of serving both elite and mass educational needs when institutions are standardized rather than diverse was described by Clark (1976) in his analysis of the severe problems faced by other nations as they try to adapt a "singular structure to plural needs" (p. 33). Clark's comment that "mass systems must be more differentiated than elite ones as they absorb a more heterogeneous clientele, respond to new demands from the labor market, and attempt to cover a wider range of knowledge" (p. 33) underscores the critical importance of institutional diversity as the key factor permitting the coexistence in one system of mass and elite values.

In considering the concepts of elite and mass higher education, it is common to relate "elite" to institutions with selective admissions policies, high tuition costs, middle and upper socioeconomic students, and high reputation. Such institutions apply a rich resource base to programs emphasizing general and liberal education. Such institutions are almost always nonpublic. Institutions of mass higher education, on the other hand, are generally considered nonselective, having low tuition, serving low socioeconomic students, and having limited resources to apply to programs that are usually vocational or technical.

Seen from this perspective, these two institutional forms can arise and coexist in a system characterized by diversity.

From another perspective, however, it can be argued that the forms' major effect is not just to supplement each other but to interact dynamically. Trow (1979), for example, argued that the "survival of elite higher education depends absolutely upon the existence of a comprehensive system of non-elite institutions" (p. 285).

Trow's argument is based upon viewing the distinctive characteristics of elite higher education not solely within the context of curriculum or student characteristics but as to their purposes and forms. In Trow's view, elite institutions attempt to socialize, not merely train; they emphasize close and prolonged relationships and interactions between students and teachers; and they attempt to raise their students' ambitions. Mass higher education, on the other hand, is concerned with the transmission of skills and knowledge related to work and life interests. Elite institutions focus upon issues of academic standards and the achievement of acceptable levels of understanding and competence, but mass institutions are increasingly adopting criteria of success based upon the concept of "value added," in which student gains are determined to be of greatest importance, even if no specified level of achievement is reached.

Although it is possible to identify certain institutions as exemplifying the major characteristics of elite or mass, in fact almost all institutions reflect, at least to some extent, the values and norms of both types. The existence of these two contradictory values creates tensions in most institutions, making it possible to establish and confirm their role in the division of academic labor and at the same time to more fully integrate their activities and values into a comprehensive higher education system. As Trow pointed out, the movement of students and faculty between elite and mass institutions would not be possible "if it were not for the active presence of elite concepts and values in the mass institutions (and conversely if certain principles of mass higher education were not accepted by the predominantly elite institutions)" (p. 281).

Without the tensions between institutional types (and in varying degrees within institutions) that arise from these two different approaches to higher education, it is doubtful whether the higher educational needs of a pluralistic industrialized society could be successfully met. A system of elite higher education without the balancing force of mass higher education would not be politically or socially viable; a system of mass higher education without the academic models and values of elite institutions would be unsound educationally and politically. Each subsystem depends upon the existence of the other; each subsystem, in turn, is based upon the existence of institutional diversity.

Facilitating Reform Through Competition. Unlike institutions in many other nations, American colleges and universities always have had to compete for scarce resources. Clark (1976) pointed out that "no other major system of higher education engages its constituent colleges and universities in so much competition. This is a natural outcome of the long struggle for institutional survival and advantage under conditions of radical decentralization. Competition has been self-generating as colleges raised their claims, took faculty and students from one another, and altered the affections and loyalties of various publics. . . . In such bad times . . . most institutions have to scramble and scrap . . . hunting for new missions and clienteles and otherwise responding to their own postures in the market" (pp. 34–35). In various times and settings, these resources have included students, financial support, community support, prestige, and faculty. The period between the end of World War II and the beginning of the 1970s was somewhat atypical of conditions in American higher education since a burgeoning student interest then resulted in a seller's market. Prior to that time, however, and increasingly since the recognition of the effects of the 1970 census upon projected college enrollments during the next decades, American higher education has been a buyer's market. Before 1950, the competition for students among diverse institutions was for many a matter of survival. This competition not only ensured that the system would remain responsive to society's changing needs (Ben-David, 1972), it also led to significant educational reform in an effort to remain attractive to students.

These reforms sometimes led to changes at individual institutions that later served as models for others. In other cases, new educational missions and orientations resulted from the competitive nature of the system, so that competition not only has been a consequence of diversity but in many ways has been a cause of it.

During the early and mid-nineteenth century, for example, colleges were proliferating at a rate well in excess of the interest of the potential applicant pool. During this period, the substitution of modern for classical languages, degree programs paralleling the B.A., the elective system, and the infusion of science and practical studies into the curriculum were adopted. Although many of these innovations had elaborate philosophical justifications, to a great extent they were developed as a means of developing new markets that would permit institutions to survive in a competitive environment. As Rudolph (1977) observed, "Since survival was always on their minds, college authorities were not purists about the course of study" (p. 83). An even more dramatic example of the impact of competition upon curriculum reform in a buyer's market is in Rudolph's description of the rationale for Francis Wayland's development of a scientific program of studies at Brown. "Apparently Brown's degree policy was dictated by Wayland's views of political economy as much as by his educational philosophy. He aimed at a curriculum that would be popular enough to pay for itself, that would be democratic in its diffusion of learning and economical in its effects on enrollments and the college's budget" (p. 109).

Not only new programs, degrees, and pedagogies developed as a result of the need to compete; new institutional missions were formed as well. Because new institutions could not compete on the basis of prestige with older established ones, they were forced to develop new missions and constituencies. Cornell's development of the concept of practical and technical programs available to everyone and the emphasis by Clark, Johns Hopkins, and Chicago upon graduate training and research were two different directions taken by new institutions in an attempt to develop new scales of prestige when they could not compete successfully on the old one (Ben-David, 1972).

The need to compete for survival has been exacerbated by predictions of undergraduate enrollment declines systemwide of up to 40 percent by 1997. Even though "best guess" estimates place the probable decline at between 5 and 15 percent, the effects upon certain types of institutions in certain parts of the country will be catastrophic (Carnegie Council, 1980). Competition for new students is likely to lead to significant innovations in curriculum, delivery systems, and administrative processes. Some innovations may be wasteful and pernicious; others may lead to effective and highly desirable reforms. These changes affect both the institutions that adopt them and others. As the Newman report (1971) stated in recommending the creation of new types of institutions with new missions, "their competition can be an important pressure for reform of the existing institutions" (p. ix).

System Arguments for Diversity

A system is defined as an "organized, unitary whole composed of two or more interdependent parts, components, or subsystems and delineated by identifiable boundaries from its environmental suprasystem" (Kast and Rosenzweig, 1973, p. 10). Within this context, "higher education" can be considered a single system consisting of individual institutions as component subsystems and embedded within a suprasystem that includes the social, political, and economic environment within which colleges and universities function.

Higher education is an "open system" exhibiting certain characteristics common to all open systems (Katz and Kahn, 1978). Among other things, the system has interactive components; is open to the environment from which it receives inputs in the form of students, money, faculty, and other resources; and engages in processes that transform these resources into outputs that are then returned to the environment. Because of these characteristics of an open system, higher education is able to function in an organized way, even in the absence of a formal coordinating structure. The development of "coordination without a coordinator" (Wildavsky, 1979, p. 90) occurs through two related processes. One process involves all components of the system accepting certain values, structures, and processes that develop over time in interaction with the environment and that uniquely come to define components as either inside or outside the system. Examples in higher education include accepted concepts of academic freedom, lay board control, and the teacher-student relationship. The environment is replete with formal and informal mechanisms (for example, voluntary accrediting groups, professional associations, directory services) that help define and reinforce these common systemic elements. The existence of universally accepted definitions, roles, and certifications throughout the system testifies to a common culture that has developed through interaction between the component units as well as through interchanges with the environment.

The second process that has created a system without the need for central coordination involves the action of the marketplace. Individual institutions (the components of the system) always have had to compete with each other for scarce resources, including money, prestige, and students. Ironically, the competition processes in which individual components engage are also a mechanism by which the system as a whole is coordinated. The development of a system so integrated that student transfer between institutions and levels is common and unremarkable is caused by the individual decisions of institutions attempting to remain competitive in a marketplace dominated by the cumulative behaviors of potential constituents.

A system requires both coordination of the whole and differentiation of the parts. Unless the components being coordinated are different in some ways, each from the other, a system does not exist. In higher education, the concept of differentiation is manifested by the existence of institutional diversity. The maintenance of the system itself therefore depends upon two factors. On one hand, there must be processes for the coordination of component units. These processes may be formalized and highly structured, as seen, for example, in states in which all public (and occasionally nonpublic) institutions are under the jurisdiction of a statewide coordinating board or consolidated governing board; they also may be informal, such as common membership in professional associations. On the other hand, there must be component diversity so that different subunits can specialize in certain activities and meet unique needs.

Diversity in higher education is critically important not only because it more effectively meets institutional and societal needs but because through differentiation of component units it leads to stability that protects the system itself. The system's ability both to respond to the pressures of the environment and to maintain its essential character and integrity is related to the existence of (1) a large number of components in the system that are (2) diverse and (3) relatively interdependent. Such "loosely coupled systems" (Weick, 1976) can be both more sensitive to and more responsive to environmental pressures than can systems with fewer components that are alike and closely interconnected. They can be more stable as well and can "survive all kinds of catastrophes . . . simply because of the enormous variety involved in them" (Boulding, 1981, p. 108).

Diversity and Evolution. Although social systems differ in many respects from biological ones, the fact that both types are open suggests that they have many similarities. Students of the development of higher education in this country have often used biological referents to describe metaphorically both the birth and death of institutions and the development of new institutional forms. Jencks and Riesman commented: "In the evolution of colleges as of species, then, order and apparent rationality emerged through natural selection and adaptation over time rather than from the initial mutations, many of which were freakish and almost random" (1977, pp. 3-4). Other observers have referred to the American situation as having "evolved out of a specific sequence of struggles" (Clark, 1976, p. 32) and noted that institutions existing today are "the survivors, the institutions that adapted to the needs of their constituencies" (Harcleroad, 1981, p. 199).

During the past ten years, social scientists and organizational sociologists have paid increasing attention to the role of the environment in influencing organizational structure and functioning. One major consequence of this consideration has been the proposal that the similarities between biological change and organizational or cultural change are not merely metaphorical but that changes that can be seen in communities of organizations over time are caused by the same interactions between organisms and environment that define the evolution of biological species. This view has been referred to as the natural selection (or population ecology) model of organizational change. It is in partial conflict with the more prevalent concept of organization-environment relations, which is called the resource dependence model. The following description of the two models points out their differences.

Resource Dependence. The resource dependence model (Scott, 1981; Pfeffer and Salancik, 1978; Hannan and Freeman, 1977) focuses upon the ability of individual organizations to constantly survey their environment to perceive changes that might pose threats or present new opportunities for survival and growth. Based upon the concept that "the key to organizational survival is the ability to acquire and maintain resources" (Pfeffer and Salancik, 1978, p. 2), the model posits active organizations that are able to develop new tactics and strategies to maintain or increase the availability of resources as the environment changes and that in many cases can actively manipulate the environment to their own advantage. Those organizations that do so successfully survive; those that do not may perish. This model is implicit in most contemporary considerations of college and university administration and management, which recommend that institutional participants adopt new tactics (new behaviors within existing structures and policies) or new strategies (changes in basic structure or policies) to cope more effectively with environmental turbulence and declining resources.

Although this model can provide valuable insights for examining the effects of the environment upon organizational change, it is not adequate for describing long-term changes in the structure of this country's higher education system. For example, it focuses upon the changes in *individual* organizations rather than in a *system* of organizations. In addition, although it recognizes that organizations can influence their environment, the model still tends to deal with short-term institutional accommodations to environmental change, some of which conceivably might be immediately productive but ultimately dysfunctional if viewed over a longer time span. It also ignores the possibility that some changes made by a small number of institutions and found effective might prove counterproductive if adopted by a large number of institutions. Of greatest importance, however, is this model's tendency to underestimate the significant difficulties faced by organizations wishing to make a major change in their structure or processes. True, some colleges and universities in fact have undertaken the strategic policy changes suggested by the resource dependence model (Anderson, 1977). However, basic changes in mission, organization, or structure are severely circumscribed in most organizations (Hannan and Freeman, 1977; Aldrich, 1979). The internal constraints include: (1) investments an organization has in the physical plant, equipment, and specialized personnel that are difficult to transfer to other functions; (2) decision makers having access to limited information, thereby limiting their ability to assess environmental changes accurately and the capability of the organization to respond to new demands; (3) political constraints within the organization that prevent the initiation of changes that may be perceived as threatening by the organization's actors; and (4) standard operating procedures and normative agreements that impede any adaptation strategies that deviate radically from the purposes for which the organization was established. External constraints include: (1) legal and fiscal barriers that make the entry and exit of organizations into the market difficult; (2) the external environment's perception of the legitimate function of the organization, which constrains it from making changes that might negate its claim to legitimacy; and (3) the fact that strategies chosen by one organization are not necessarily functional for other similar organizations (Hannan and Freeman, 1977).

In higher education, for example, changes in basic form are constrained by a number of internal and external factors, such as legal requirements, socialization patterns of faculty and administration, expectations of important constituent groups, and policies such as tenure, which limit organizational flexibility. A church-related, liberal arts junior college might see the great opportunities available if it could become publicly supported and offer graduate work in the health sciences, but both internal and external constraints would make such strategic policy changes highly improbable.

Natural Selection. The natural selection model (Scott, 1981; Hannan and Freeman, 1977; Aldrich, 1979; Campbell, 1975; Aldrich and Pfeffer, 1976; Campbell, 1969) is based upon the natural selection model of biological ecology. Campbell (1969) developed the concept of the relationship "between biological evolution and the selective propagation of cultural forms" (p. 73), which has since been developed to look specifically at changes in organizations (Aldrich, 1979; Hannan and Freeman, 1977; Aldrich and Pfeffer, 1976). The model proposes that the environment acts in such a way as to select certain types of organizations for survival, based upon the fit between the particular characteristics of the environment and the form of the organization. As the characteristics of the environment change, it would be expected that organizational forms would change as well.

The model is concerned with populations of organizations (that is, "aggregates of organizations that are alike in some respect" [Scott, 1981, p. 171]) rather than individual institutions. Therefore, it looks not at how individual organizations may change over time but at the selective propagation of changes in large populations of organizations (Aldrich and Pfeffer, 1976). Organizations are seen as evolving, as do biological species, through a three-stage sequential process of variation, selection, and retention. The consequence of the process is that in the competition for scarce resources, those organizations that are most "fit" are those that survive. In the case of organizations, as in the case of biology, "fitness" does not imply that surviving organizations are more advanced or in other ways necessarily "better" than those that do not, only that they are more adapted to existing environmental conditions. Primarily through this distinction can the natural selection model be intellectually distinguished from the earlier and discredited notion of social Darwinism, which was based upon the notions of progress, purpose, and the survival of the fittest. Believing that reality moves toward more perfect states, social Darwinists were able to justify the injustices of the existing social order by citing it as an example of the wisdom of nature (Aldrich, 1979).

Variation, the first stage in the process, is manifested in the higher education system through institutional diversity. Only if there is a wide variety of forms can natural selection function; "the general principle is that the greater the heterogeneity and the number of variations, the more the opportunities for a close fit to environmental selection criteria" (Aldrich, 1979, p. 35). The remarkable responsiveness of American higher education to society's needs can be seen, based upon this model, as depending upon the constant availability of a great number of different institutions exhibiting different forms, processes, and characteristics.

Variations can be introduced into the system in a number of ways, including the development of innovations in existing organizations and the creation of new organizations. Some of these variations can be planned; in other cases, they may arise randomly, through error, or as unforeseen consequences of institutional plans or activities. In organizations with relatively few standardized procedures, the cumulation of random errors repeated and combined can introduce sizable variation in organizational functioning over time (Aldrich, 1979); it should be expected that such sources of variation would be particularly noticeable in colleges and universities. Although in many ways unplanned variation may be even more important than planned differences, the process of natural selection is itself indifferent to the cause; the only critical element is that there be variation through whatever means. Natural selection cannot proceed in a system consisting of uniform elements (Aldrich and Pfeffer, 1976).

The second stage of the process is *selection.* Through the competition for resources, those organizations that more closely match the requirements of the environment survive, while those that do not are negatively selected and fail. Environmental resources may be of many kinds, but because the budgets of almost all institutions in this country are either enrollment-driven or enrollment-related, the most critical resource for most institutions is the number of students they can attract. The independent liberal arts college, the proprietary technical college, and the four-year community college are examples of the diversity of institutional types that comprise the institutional variation essential to an evolutionary process and illustrate the effects of natural selection. The three types of institutions all had to face the competition of other institutions as well as the changing social, political, and economic environment that provided both opportunities for resources and constraints to growth. During the past twenty years, the independent liberal arts colleges increasingly have come under pressure from the development of low-cost, public, comprehensive institutions; until recently, proprietary technical colleges were denied the right to receive accreditation or award degrees; the four-year community college (grades 11 to 14) was developed in California in the late 1930s and early 1940s and competed with existing two-year colleges.

In the third stage, *retention,* those organizational forms that succeed are preserved over time, and other organizations of the same form may be created. As the environment changes, the fitness of an organization may be altered as other forms are selected by the environment as being more adaptable to the new environmental demands. The three institutional types used as examples were each selected differently for retention. The independent liberal arts college was positively selected, and it has remained a strong component of the system up to the present time. Its future in a changing environment is uncertain. The four-year community college did not fare as well. Although scholars at the end of World War II said, "the four-year junior college will become the prevailing type of junior college orientation" (Sexson and Harbeson, 1946, p. 297), these community colleges were negatively selected by the environment (one major constraint being their inability to field athletic teams eligible to play either high schools or colleges) and shortly thereafter disappeared. The prospects of the proprietary technical college in the retention phase are still unclear because of the recency of the phenomenon. Many of the original organizations still exist, and other organizations of the same form have been created, indicating the possibility of positive selection in the contemporary environment. But it is difficult to predict the course of evolution because of the indeterminate nature of the environment. Within the next twenty years, proprietary institutions could flourish and expand in an environment of decreased public funding, or they could shrivel and disappear in the competition with community colleges offering similar programs at lower cost.

Both the resource dependence and the natural selection models agree upon the importance of the environment as a factor explaining organizational survival and change. Because this study is concerned with changes in the system of higher education over time, rather than with changes in any particular institution, it adopts the natural selection perspective. Campbell (1975) suggested that it is "the only and all-purpose explanation for the achievement of fit between systems and for the achievement and maintenance of counterentropic form and order" (p. 1105). Although there are reasons why the natural selection model may not be as fully applicable to organizational systems as to biological ones (see the appendix), the model appears generally suited to studying the effects of the environment upon colleges and universities. Scott (1981) commented: "The natural selection perspective is more readily applied to relatively small and numerous organizations that are not individually in a position to exert much effect on their environments. The approach can usefully be applied to such organizations as colleges" (p. 205).

Diversity and Niches. Evolution, whether of biological or social organisms, occurs through the filling of niches within an ecosystem. To a biologist, a niche can be defined as the place or role of a species in a community, as "part of the whole set of relationships of the species to the environment" (Whittaker and Levin, 1975, p. 2). To a student of organizations, a niche is "all those combinations of resource levels at which the population can survive and reproduce itself" (Hannan and Freeman, 1977, p. 974).

Niches arise out of various combinations of physical, biological, psychological, and social conditions that provide resources or establish constraints to organizations. "A niche is created by the intersection of resource constraints–an abstract resource space consisting of a unique combination of resources (information, access to materials, customers, and so on) that could permit a form to survive there. Forms thus take advantage of a niche's resource space" (Aldrich, 1979, p. 40). Evolution occurs as organizations seek their resources within available niches; those most fitted to a particular niche survive, and those less suited either fail or must discover another niche in which they can function.

From the perspective of colleges and universities, niches are created primarily by the interaction of factors that result in conscious and unconscious choices made by various potential organizational constituencies, including consumers, participants, donors, politicians, and other major groups. Boulding (1981) pointed out that niches in economic systems differ from those in biological ones because they are determined primarily by the willingness of people to purchase commodities in them. For example, the existence in the environment of a large number of middle-class, career-oriented recent high school graduates interested in full-time study in nonresidential settings, coupled with general public support for higher education, offers a potential organizational niche that might be filled by a number of different types of institutions, including regional state colleges, comprehensive independent institutions, institutions with nominal sectarian affiliation, or community colleges. All other factors being equal, the type of institution that potential constituents are most willing to support by purchasing services will most closely "fit" this niche; the others may not survive unless they can find other niches that can provide adequate resources. Such niches may be differentiated from others by the presence of students who live in specific locations, who share common cultural backgrounds and interests, or who exhibit a level of academic performance not seen in the niche of the dominant institutional type.

Niches have a number of major characteristics that are important to a consideration of the evolution of college and university types. First, niches are unique combinations of resources that offer the *potential* for supporting institutions. The existence of a niche does not necessarily mean that the niche will be filled. Empty niches exist in every ecosystem, and evolution occurs as institutions evolve to fill them. For example, the unique combination of adults eager to utilize their previous experiences as a basis for preparing for involvement in social activism, coupled with the availability of public grants to support such individuals, created a niche that went unrecognized until the founding of the College of Human Services.

Second, niches themselves evolve over time as environmental constraints change and as the distribution of organizations within the system changes. Niches that existed in the past because of the availability of support for veterans (and lack of effective control over the use of the support), for example, have now all but disappeared, and the institutions that had occupied such niches failed along with them. And as the constituencies that provide resources to the large population of comprehensive community colleges increase, niches once available for other types of institutions, such as private junior colleges, shrink. The principle is that "the niche of one species cannot change without changing the niches of all others in the ecosystem" (Boulding, 1981, p. 33).

Third, biological species (and by analogy institutional types) can coexist only if they occupy different niches. The principle of competitive exclusion states that "if two species are limited by the availability of the same single resource at the same time and place in the same stable community, one of these species will have the advantage and the other will become extinct" (Whittaker and Levin, 1975, p. 3). This principle indicates the critical effect of the availability of different niches upon species diversity: The greater the number of niches, the greater the number of distinctive institutional types that can be supported by the environment.

Because the principle of competitive exclusion is framed in terms of a stable community, it might be expected that its effects would not be seen dramatically in a situation in which the growth of resources outstrips the ability of species to exploit them. Indeed, the excess availability of potential college students and funding resources during the period roughly between 1950 and 1970 may have made it possible for two institutional species to occupy the same niche and for both to prosper. As higher education moves from its current "steady state" to one of declining resources, the coexistence of two different types of institutions (for example, the nonselective state college and the local community college) in the same niche will no longer be possible. The consequences of the functioning of competitive exclusion is discussed in greater detail in Chapter Seven.

Fourth, environmental developments and constraints have a major effect upon the size and availability of niches. Recent societal changes supporting, for example, civil rights, the women's movement, and increased access for new learners have created new niches in which external degree programs and newly created, predominantly minority institutions could flourish. On the other hand, present legal constraints prohibit a niche in which a governmental body provides funds for a sectarian program. In both cases, changes in the environment could abruptly change the characteristics or viability of the niches and thus the distribution of institutions within them.

Zammuto's summary (1982) nicely captured the concept of niche: "In short, niches are the confluence of conditions which allow something to happen in terms of evolution. Niches create evolutionary potential which may or may not be fulfilled. As the conditions which created a particular niche change, the niche itself may be modified or closed. The conditions which create a niche and a particular evolutionary potential also provide boundaries as to what is possible at any given time. While conditions may arise which allow the evolution of a biological or social form, they also define the limits of growth that those forms can take. The constant process of changing physical, biological, and social conditions creates the backdrop against which evolution occurs" (p. 61).

Diversity and "Waste." Ehrlich (1979) argued the need for diversity in both biological communities and human culture. He pointed out that the living components of the natural ecological system are millions of species of organisms on earth. The species' interaction, in ways not always understood, establishes the complex yet predictable cycles upon which life itself depends. The complexity of the system requires specialization, which is provided by species diversity, with each species occupying a distinctive ecological niche.

Niches change as both the environment and populations change in size and genetic form, but the effects of changes in niches upon the entire system are difficult to predict. Ehrlich cautioned that "Lacking full understanding of the earth's ecosystem computers but knowing they are essential to human life, ecologists tend to take a conservative view of their disruption. While it is true that removing certain components and altering others may not lethally disrupt the functioning of the system, the state of knowledge at the present moment does not, in most cases, allow prediction of what can be safely disturbed. Indeed the only general prediction that can be made is that if enough components are deleted or altered, eventually the entire system will collapse" (1979, p. 5). Species diversity must be maintained to ensure the specialized functions upon which the system depends and to prevent the unpredictable breakdown of the system if a critical element (whose critical nature cannot be known in advance) is removed.

In addition to diversity of species, the ecosystem also relies upon genetic variability *within* species. It is this variability that allows species to evolve in response to environmental change. If genetic variability within a species is reduced, as has happened in many plants as part of the development of high-yield crops, the species' vulnerability to unpredictable new enemies increases.

The ecosystem therefore relies upon two major factors: (1) the availability of a large number of differentiated species that perform unique functions in complex and unknown cycles of interaction and (2) genetic variability within species that permits evolution in response to changing environmental demands. The reduction of either factor may lead to systemic disruption and in extreme cases, ultimate system collapse.

Ehrlich believes that the same types of forces are applicable to an understanding of social as well as biological systems.

"Cultural diversity can be thought of as an analogue of genetic diversity—just as differences among genes are the raw material upon which biological evolution works, differences in the body of non-genetic information (that is, culture) possessed by individuals and societies can be thought of as the raw materials of cultural evolution. . . . In the face of what little *is* known about cultural evolution, it would seem wise for humanity to take a conservative position to the preservation of cultural resources for the same sorts of reasons that commend a conservative approach to the preservation of biological diversity" (1979, pp. 9-10).

Translating these ideas to the higher education system suggests the need for a diversity of both institutional forms (species) and approaches to problems within institutions of the same type (genetic variability), if the system itself is to evolve over time and minimize its vulnerability to changes in the environment. The variability of institutional forms was discussed in relation to natural selection. Genetic variability in biology is related to genetic instructions carried in the cell itself. In the case of organizations, the genetic instructions are contained in other social artifacts (Boulding, 1981), such as institutional regulations, flowcharts, planning documents, and similar materials. Genetic variability would be seen in community colleges, for example, if different institutions attempted, while retaining their organizational form, to utilize different instructional technologies (such as CAI, audiotutorials, newspaper courses, lectures), develop unusual programs (such as fisheries technology, casino technology), try nontraditional management practices (for example, collective bargaining, MBO, term contracts), and in other ways experiment with different approaches that in the future could increase their environmental fitness.

An even more provocative consequence of comparing biological and social systems is an understanding of the role of waste and mutation in reducing systemic vulnerability and increasing adaptation. In biological systems, mutation is a source of waste in which profligate nature randomly produces changes whose usefulness in survival is determined through the processes of natural selection. Most mutations are nonviable, but which will survive and which will not can be determined retrospectively and not in advance. A natural biological system functions effectively because a large number of "experiments" are attempted, only a few of which are able to survive in the competition for resources. "Waste, in the Darwinian scheme, not only produces progress but also conserves the advances already made. There is no heredity without tax of mutation; most mutations are bad; their production and elimination are a kind of waste. The sentimentalist who seeks to eliminate the waste in a species by preserving all mutants and breeding equally of all genetic types ultimately brings about the extinction of the entire species. It is a throwing of good money after bad. It is the saving of pawns and losing the game" (Hardin, 1959, pp. 308–309).

To survive, not only must a system be able to engage in "wasteful" practices, it must also ensure that variability is not decreased by placing an emphasis upon one form that, at any specific time, appears the most useful. "Any species that becomes one big melting pot of genes puts—to mix metaphors—all its eggs in one basket. If circumstances change rapidly, it may be unable to adapt, and so will perish" (Hardin, 1959, p. 309).

Hardin presented these ideas in the chapter "In Praise of Waste," and in the higher education system, these same considerations have led some to praise inefficiency (Boulding, 1978), to recognize the system's need for organizational slack (Trow, 1979), and to recommend that opportunities for new enterprises be kept available even during a no- or low-growth period (Carnegie Foundation, 1976).

It is important to recognize that not all, perhaps not even most, of these "experiments" can be rationally planned and evaluated. Social evolution, Campbell (1975) pointed out, is "a process in which adaptive belief systems could be accumulated which none of its innovators, transmitters, or participants properly understood, a tradition wiser than any of the persons transmitting it" (p. 1107). If the system is to work, it must pass along not only those innovations that may later prove critical for species survival but many other nonadaptive and potentially dysfunctional processes and behaviors. "The retention system, not being omniscient, is powerless to tell dross from gold; it must dutifully hang on to both" (p. 1107).

The maintenance of the system therefore depends upon both the encouragement of institutional diversity (organizational form) and varying solutions to institutional problems (genetic variability). The system must support not only institutions recognized as being important to meet contemporary needs but the opportunity for the development of institutions with different structures, purposes, clienteles, or technologies that can have a chance to compete for survival. There is no basis for judging in advance the possible future value of such unorthodox experiments, or "mutations"; if they are to be judged at all, only contemporary standards can be applied. Institutional diversity is thus an investment in an uncertain future, an investment that the system as a whole cannot afford not to make.

Diversity and Institutional Survival. Preservation of the system does not necessarily imply the survival of each of the system's components. Except when the components exist in a placid environment, or under conditions of extreme systemwide slack, it would be expected that some existing components would be eliminated and some new ones created in response to changing environmental demands. Because for most of its existence the higher education system's capacity has far exceeded the demand, the primary mechanism through which this process of institutional birth and death has occurred has been the marketplace.

The survival rate of organizational components of systems outside higher education suggests that this process is not uncommon. It was reported, for example, that federal government bureaus "die" annually at a rate of 28 per 10,000 and that the comparable annual rate for business organizations is 57 per 10,000 (Katz and Kahn, 1978, p. 81). The most comparable data for institutions of higher education are those prepared by Zammuto (1983a) indicating a mortality rate of 98.6 per 10,000 between 1971 and 1981. Historically, it was reported that the annual mortality of colleges and universities between 1770 and 1870 was 6.5, which, based upon the 891 institutions founded during that period, works out to a rate of approximately 72 per 10,000. The mortality of private four-year colleges between 1970 and 1975 was calculated at the annual rate of 50 per 10,000, although the rate would have been higher had private two-year institutions also been included (Bowen and Minter, 1975, p. 72). Tewksbury (1932) reported that 700 colleges failed in this country before the Civil War. And the trends of that time persist. Trow (1979) commented that "The extraordinary phenomenon of high fertility and high mortality rates among institutions of higher learning is still with us. Between 1969 and 1975, some 800 new colleges (many of them community colleges) were created, while roughly 300 were closed or consolidated, leaving a net gain of nearly 500 in just six years. . . . And this points to the very strong link between higher education in the United States and the mechanisms of the market. This link to the market was and still is a major factor in the emergence and persistence of large numbers and diverse forms of colleges and universities in America" (p. 272).

In reviewing the Bowen and Minter data, Finn (1978) suggested the possibility that the mortality rates may be "too *low* to make room for the entry of the new institutions needed for a truly dynamic industry" (p. 42). The closing of institutions is thus an indication that higher education "shows signs of continuing dynamics, of being an industry in which marginal institutions fail but are replaced by new entrants perhaps better attuned to the changing demands of the educational marketplace" (p. 41). Maintenance of the total system has required that institutions be allowed to fail so that new and more diversified institutional forms can develop and compete openly in the marketplace for resources and support. The development of new structures and programmatic emphasis such as the technical institute, state university, land-grant college, normal school, municipal college, and community college can be seen as arising "as a response to the failure of existing institutions to meet the demands for a new or additional type of educational experience" (Brick, 1963, p. 1).

Seen from an institutional perspective, a commitment to diversity might suggest the need for the system to provide additional resources so that an otherwise nonviable college might survive. From a system perspective, however, diversity is enhanced as less adapted institutions succumb and are replaced by new and more attractive variations. The system's interests are often much different than its components' summated interests, and in the case of diversity, institutional and system solutions are not only nonidentical but in fact often diametrically opposed. Had not the system perspective been the more dominant over the history of higher education, the system itself might have collapsed or been incorporated into a small component of a different and more responsive educational system. "Evolution proceeds indeed by the endangering and the eventual extinction of species and by their replacement by others that find niches" (Boulding, 1981, p. 19).

2

What Makes Institutions Different?

Although the concept of "institutional diversity" is one of the ideological pillars of American higher education, there is no commonly accepted definition that permits it to be used analytically. Among different persons or representatives of special constituencies, the concept has been used variously to refer to increased student access to postsecondary education, the protection of colleges in the private sector, institutional autonomy in state systems, heterogeneity in the ethnic or socioeconomic mix of campus enrollments, the availability of a larger selection of programs and degrees in individual institutions, the geographical dispersion of institutions, and so on. Failure to define the concept in operational terms has resulted quite naturally in disagreement about the present level of institutional diversity in this country, the extent to which diversity is increasing or decreasing, and even the reasons why diversity is important in a system of higher education.

Internal and External Diversity

Part of the confusion in defining diversity stems from a failure to distinguish between internal and external differentiation. Internal diversity is differentiation of mission, program, clienteles, instructional methodology or delivery system, structures, or other characteristics *within a single institution* (Stadtman, 1980, p. 98). Internal diversity therefore would be enhanced if an institution with a teaching mission also embraced a research orientation, an institution with selective admissions requirements decided to also enroll underprepared students, a college implemented a program of audiotutorial instruction to complement its traditional reliance upon lecture-recitation techniques, or a traditional liberal arts institution added an MBA program to its curriculum.

Many, perhaps most, of the changes leading to internal diversity are responses to political, social, economic, and demographic factors in the external environment and outside the control of the institutions affected. A more complete analysis of these factors, and their effects upon diversity, is presented in a later section. But even a cursory look at the growth of job-related programs and other changes in programs developed by institutions in response to the increased enrollments of older students, women, low-achieving students, ethnic minorities, and other "new learners" (Cross, 1976) suggests that many institutions are becoming more internally diverse.

Perhaps the archetypical example of internal diversity in American higher education is the multiversity—an institution of incredible size and complexity that simultaneously embraces so many different purposes and different constituencies that "it must, of necessity, be partially at war with itself" (Kerr, 1964, p. 9). As other institutions increase in size and begin to diversify program and clienteles, either under the pressure of projected enrollment declines or in response to the interests of their existing student body, increasingly they may come to share the internal diversification of the multiversity. The community college (which perhaps not coincidentally is, like the multiversity, a distinctly American invention) has already done so, and there are such institutions that rival the multiversity in size, complexity, responsiveness to different constituencies, and internal complexity, if not in prestige.

As institutions with previously distinctive characteristics become more internally diversified, they may tend to become somewhat more alike and less different from each other. For example, if a liberal arts college adds a degree program in business and a support program for disadvantaged students, while an urban community college develops two-year transfer programs and a general education core, both schools become not only more diversified themselves, they come to share characteristics that previously were unique to each. For this reason, internal diversity is not only *different* from institutional diversity, it in fact may be correlated negatively with it. The implications of increased internal diversity for changes in institutional diversity are discussed later in this chapter.

Internal diversity refers to differences *within* institutions; external or institutional diversity refers to differences *between* institutions. Stadtman (1980) defined diversity as "a condition of having differences, and in higher education it characterizes any system in which individual institutions or groups of institutions differ from one another in any way. But that definition applies to several, often overlapping types of diversity. It can be programmatic, procedural, systemic, constituential, or reputational—to suggest only a few of its forms" (p. 97). To these types may be added at least one other: diversity of structure.

The various forms of external diversity suggested by Stadtman have been considered in a number of studies and research reports. A majority focus upon one diversity form only, paying only peripheral attention to the others, although in many cases the forms are highly intercorrelated. A brief survey of the literature provides a better understanding of the dimensions of each form and an appreciation of the different definitions that have been used to describe the characteristics of these external differences.

Programmatic Diversity

Institutions can be distinguished on at least five programmatic bases: degree level, degree area, comprehensiveness, mission, and emphasis. Although many institutions offer nondegree work that is central to their mission, ranging from certificate programs in community colleges to postdoctoral appointments in major research universities, most students in institutions of higher education are pursuing degrees at one of four levels. The associate degree (usually the associate in arts, science, or applied science) is offered as the highest degree in almost all public community and private junior colleges. Although in the past the Carnegie Commission (1971a) recommended that four-year colleges and universities use the associate degree as an interim incentive for students studying for the baccalaureate, as well as a credential for those who do not wish to complete the full four-year program, this recommendation has not been widely adopted. Therefore, the associate degree by and large is a unique programmatic emphasis of public and private two-year institutions.

The baccalaureate degree, traditionally the bachelor of arts or bachelor of science but increasingly including professional and specialized degrees (for example, bachelor of music, bachelor of general studies, bachelor of social work), is offered by almost all institutions that do not award the associate degree. In some of these institutions, the baccalaureate is the highest degree offered. In an increasing number of institutions, however, the highest degree awarded is at the master's level, usually in a professional area. The proliferation of professional master's degrees at institutions that formerly had offered only the baccalaureate has led to an almost incomprehensible jumble of degree nomenclatures to supplement the time-honored (if loosely defined) master of arts and master of science.

A relatively small number of institutions offer the doctor of philosophy or doctor of education as their highest degrees, to a lesser extent also using additional designations to reflect doctoral work in specialized professional areas (for example, doctor of social work, doctor of arts, doctor of psychology).

Defining institutions based upon the highest degree offered—associate, bachelor's, master's, doctor's—is one way of representing the institutional diversity that captures almost all institutions of higher education, with the exception of a small number of stand-alone professional schools that might, for example, offer only the doctor of medicine (M.D.) or doctor of law (J.D.), both of which somewhat confuse the picture by being commonly referred to as a "doctorate" but really considered a "first professional degree." Based upon the criterion of degree level offered, therefore, institutional diversity would be decreased as colleges attempted to expand their degree-level offerings by adding degree programs at either a higher or lower level (although internal diversity would increase).

A separate, although probably related, area of programmatic diversity is defined by the areas in which degrees are offered. Although there are no universally recognized categories for such areas, probably most program offerings could be subsumed under the general groupings of liberal arts, professional, technical, or religious, with an almost infinite and constantly changing variety of specializations or majors within each group. However, even these categories themselves become confusing as programs with ostensibly the same name differ in substance and those with apparently different identifications become subtly, and then overtly, more alike. Programs identified as "liberal arts" that have incorporated within them distinctly vocational components, for example, become increasingly difficult to classify or to separate from programs with unabashed professional intentions.

The aggregation of programs within an institution permits classification according to the third programmatic variable: comprehensiveness. Although institutions can be more or less comprehensive, the simplest distinction is between those institutions with a single curriculum orientation and those with more than one. Examples of the former are the traditional liberal arts college, teacher's college, or technical school. Examples of the latter include institutions with more than two types of programs, such as a single comprehensive college or community college offering a mix of liberal arts, professional, and technical curricula. For various reasons that are elaborated later in this study, institutions are likely to move away from single-purpose toward comprehensiveness rather than the reverse, thus contributing again to internal diversity at the expense of institutional diversity.

Institutional mission constitutes the fourth programmatic

element of diversity. Early formulations presented a trilogy of possible missions for institutions of higher education: teaching, research, and service. Some institutions can be identified as focusing primarily upon only one of these orientations (for example, the overriding concern of the traditional liberal arts college for teaching). Others give significant attention to two orientations (the community college), and still others mix all three (the flagship state university). More recently, considerations of the higher education system's purposes as a whole, as well as the relative emphasis upon the purposes by individual institutions consistent with a sense of mission, have identified five major goal areas: educating students, advancing human capability in society at large, assisting with the provision of educational justice, providing an effective locus for pure scholarship and artistic creativity, and providing an effective locus for the evaluation of society (Carnegie Commission, 1973b). Each purpose is related to a series of activities—some of which are performed on most campuses, others of which may take place on relatively few—including such functions or processes as general education, personal support, research, service, vocational training, remedial programs, financial aid, and resources for pure scholarship, the unique combinations of which define operationally an institution's mission.

Closely related to the issue of mission in a macro sense is the fifth programmatic dimension of external diversity, emphasis, which is "mission" in a micro sense. The concept of program emphasis can be more easily described than defined, but its major characteristic is that it distinguishes an institution not from those different from itself but from those that in most other respects are similar to it. One example is an institution with a distinct curriculum focus or orientation, such as an "urban mission" of the University of Wisconsin-Milwaukee or the ecological orientation of the University of Wisconsin-Green Bay. Another example is those institutions characterized by programmatic reforms that emphasize goals and values opposed to those of the university college model, such as the neoclassical reforms of St. John's at Annapolis, the activist-radical programs of the College for Human Services, and the activities of other institutions that resulted from what Grant and Riesman called "telic movements" (Grant and Riesman, 1978).

The concept of programmatic diversity therefore turns out to be rather complex, relating not only to the issues of what is taught, at what level, and in what combinations but to their integration into both a major mission orientation and an emphasis that may in some institutions become those colleges' single most identifiable characteristic.

Procedural Diversity

Programmatic diversity refers to *what* is offered; procedural diversity is related to *how* it is offered. At least three types of procedural diversity can be identified: delivery systems, student policies, and administrative processes.

Today, as in the past, the dominant mode of delivering educational services in higher education is based upon student-faculty interaction in the form of lectures, recitations, and laboratories. At the same time, there are few campuses that have not experimented in some degree with new forms of delivering educational services. Many of these forms rely upon the availability of new technologies or pedagogical insights, such as computer-assisted instruction, computer-managed instruction, audiotutorial instruction, and other self-paced approaches. Other forms attempt to integrate more fully the curriculum and the environment, as exemplified by work study programs, to reduce reliance upon the direct student-faculty relationship through independent study, or to make use of resources off campus through study abroad or sharing of campus resources. On most campuses, these atypical approaches to the delivery of education are at such a low level and of such peripheral importance to the institutions' mission that their presence has almost no impact upon institutional diversity. In a small number of instances, however, such changes are adopted at a level high enough to significantly affect all other aspects of college functioning and therefore can be clearly considered as contributing to external diversity. Examples include LaGuardia Community College, which requires all students in all programs to participate in several months-long work study assignments; Empire State College, which negotiates learning contracts with a mature student body who then implement an individualized sequence of off-campus learning activities; Nova University, which prepares materials for study in off-campus sites by groups of students who are visited once a month by traveling faculty; the New York State Regents External Degree Program and Edison College of New Jersey, which offer degrees based upon portfolio assessment and performance on proficiency examinations of nontraditional students; and Friends World College, which holds no classes and requires students to study four years at off-campus sites.

Student policies, particularly those aimed at aspects of academic life, are another source of possible diversity. As is the case of modifications in delivery systems, however, many of the more recently adopted student and academic policies reflect general trends in American higher education and for the most part impart no particular distinctiveness to those institutions that have adopted some of them. The policies include what Grant and Riesman (1978) referred to as "popular reforms," such as student-designed majors, interdisciplinary programs, new grading systems, student-initiated courses, and other "innovations" that have increased student options and institutional flexibility. In a few cases, however, academic policies have been altered to create a program so different from that of other institutions that it has made a contribution to external diversity; for example, the development of a competency-based curriculum at Alverno College.

For the most part, administrative policies are so indirectly related to institutional programs and so constricted by the exigencies of the external environment that their procedures usually do not differ widely at different institutions, and they have little if any effect upon the institution even when they do. There are cases, however, of administrative provisions that can, by interacting with other campus variables, create sets of organizational programs that contribute to external diversity. The University of Wisconsin-Oshkosh's adoption of a modular academic calendar coupled with a computer-driven system of continuous registration made registration and scheduling more efficient (by itself of little direct importance) and also led to changes in faculty responsibilities, student programming, and delivery system mix, creating distinctive institutional processes. Blackburn College's requirement that all students contribute fifteen hours a week to the operation of the college not only helps reduce tuition but significantly changes the climate of the campus and affects the educational program.

Procedural diversity can be extended to consider additional factors such as college policies related to tenure, but as such factors become further removed from the educational program, their impact upon institutional functioning becomes less noticeable. Generally, the contributions of procedural differences to institutional diversity are minor compared to the impact of programmatic diversity.

Systemic Diversity

The concept of systemic diversity refers to differences in institutional type, size, and control. These are the variables most often considered when dealing with the concept of diversity, and they are closely related to the other forms of diversity presented in this chapter as well as to each other.

There have been numerous attempts to categorize colleges and universities by institutional type. Baldridge and others, for example, created a typology with eight categories (1978); Smart (1978) clustered all institutions into five types. Other typologies were developed by Astin (1962), Bowen and Minter (1976), Ladd and Lipset (1975), and Lazersfeld and Thielens (1958). The most widely employed classification, however, was developed by the Carnegie Council (1976) and divides institutions into six major categories and nineteen subcategories based upon several criteria, including level of federal financial support, degree offering, undergraduate selectivity, program, and institutional size. The six major categories are (1) doctoral-granting institutions (subdivided into four groups based upon level of federal support and number of degrees awarded), (2) comprehensive colleges and universities (subdivided into two groups based upon program and enrollment), (3) liberal arts colleges (subdivided into two groups based upon their admissions standards or the number of graduates later earning the doctorate), (4) two-year colleges or institutions, (5) professional schools and other specialized institutions (subdivided into nine groups based upon program), and (6) institutions for nontraditional study. The most well-known institutions in the country are likely to be found in only two of the nineteen subgroups (Research Universities I, a subcategory of the doctoral-granting institutions, which includes the fifty institutions with the greatest federal support of academic science; and Liberal Arts Colleges I, a subcategory of liberal arts colleges with selective admissions policies). It is important to note, however, that these two subgroups constitute only a small minority of institutions in this country.

The Carnegie classification, as well as other attempts to categorize institutions by types, uses size as one defining variable. But the separation of institutions into several categories fails to capture the immense range of institutional size. In the fall of 1978, for example, the National Center for Education Statistics (1980b) reported 3,131 institutions of higher education and branches (p. 109). Of these institutions, 668 (21 percent) enrolled fewer than 500 students, and 84 (3 percent) enrolled 20,000 students or more. Enrollment in the median institution was somewhat greater than 1,300. Most institutions are relatively small, but most students are enrolled in the larger ones so the mean institutional enrollment was approximately 3,600 (headcount) students.

The third major systemic variable is control, referring to the institution's source of legal authority. To the traditional dichotomy of public and private control has been added more recently a third category of proprietary institutions, authorized in some jurisdictions to award degrees. However, even this division into three groups does not do full justice to the range of diversity in control. Public institutions may fall under state, local, state and local, or federal control, or they may be identified as "state-related." Private institutions can be identified as independent/nonprofit, proprietary (profit-making), or religiously controlled (National Center for Education Statistics, 1979). Institutions under religious control can be divided still further, based upon major group (the greatest number are under the control of various Protestant denominations, followed by Roman Catholic, Jewish, and "other" religious auspices). The concept of religious "control" can in turn be divided into categories ranging from institutions directly managed by religious orders to those whose religious affiliation, although once quite important, is now nominal (Pace, 1972; Hobbs and Meeth, 1980). In addition, some "religious" institutions are not under religious control (Cuninggim, 1978), thus adding to the complexity of the situation.

Although each of the three systemic sources of diversity can be considered separately, in many instances they are closely interrelated. Almost all small institutions and almost all liberal arts colleges are private, for example, and almost all larger institutions are public; most research universities are large. These relationships make the Carnegie classification groupings plausible in terms of certain characteristics related to diversity. Regarding other diversity characteristics, however, there are significant differences among institutions in any one of Carnegie's nineteen subcategories as well as between institutions in different categories.

Constituential Diversity

Stadtman (1980) suggested that constituential diversity is related to differences in "the family backgrounds, abilities, preparation, values, and educational goals of students" (p. 97). To this list, student factors such as sex and ethnic group identification can also be added. Note, however, that students are only one constituent of a college or university; others include the faculty and administration and the board of control, which often represents the interests of a defined political, religious, or ethnic group.

All institutions of course differ to some extent as to the distribution of the characteristics of students and other constituent groups. For many institutions, however, these differences become a distinguishing characteristic—sometimes the *most* distinguishing one. For the most part, such institutions are what Jencks and Riesman (1977) referred to as "special interest colleges" (p. 3). In contrast to the colleges of the eighteenth century, which served generally similar constituencies (although with different religious backgrounds), the special-interest colleges were created in response to the ways nineteenth-century Americans began to differentiate themselves. "By 1900 there were special colleges for Baptists and Catholics, for men and women, for whites and blacks, for rich and not-so-rich, for North and South, for small town and big city, for adolescents and adults, for engineers and teachers" (p. 3). Many of these characteristics typify some colleges today, and at least seven sources of constituential diversity can be identified: sex, ethnic identification, religion, socioeconomic status, academic ability, values and institutional climate, and geography.

As late as 1950, approximately one third of all colleges and universities enrolled only men or only women. By 1978, however, 92 percent of all institutions were coeducational (National Center for Education Statistics, 1979). Of the remainder, 111 schools were for men only, 117 were for women only, and 11 were designated as coordinate (that is, separate campuses for men and women but the campuses administered as a single institution). As would be expected, all but two of the single-sex institutions were under private control. In addition to colleges that enroll only students of the same sex, some institutions designated coeducational in fact enroll primarily students of one sex. Examples include the United States Military Academy, whose enrollment is 94 percent male, and Sarah Lawrence College, 80 percent of whose students are women.

Among colleges serving identifiable ethnic groups, the most prominent are those established for, or primarily serving, black students. These institutions have strong ties to the black community and claim special program orientations, purposes, and outcomes that relate to their students' special needs and interests (McGrath, 1965; Bowles and DeCosta, 1971; Willie and Edmonds, 1978; Jencks and Riesman, 1977). In 1976, there were 145 institutions and branches attended predominantly by black students (National Center for Education Statistics, 1980b). A majority of these institutions were public, and although many were founded after the Civil War, and later in the nineteenth century in response to the provisions of the second Morrill Act of 1890, several have been established within the past twenty years to serve constituencies in primarily urban settings. Such older institutions include Fisk University and Florida Agricultural and Mechanical University; newly established black institutions include Medgar Evers College of the City University of New York and Nairobi College.

Although predominantly black institutions constitute a majority of those colleges serving specific ethnic groups, they are by no means the only such institutions. A number of colleges recently have been created in response to the felt needs of specific ethnic interests. Some of these institutions relate to identifiable subgroups within the context of a large multicampus system, such as Hostos Community College in City University of New York, whose students are predominantly Hispanic. Others are community based, such as Navajo Community College or Universidad Boricua (Gittell and Dollar, 1975).

Religion has been a major element in the diversification of institutions in this country since the founding of the original colonial colleges. A majority of nonpublic institutions began under religious auspices, and as of 1978, 780 colleges and universities were identified as being under the control of a religious group (National Center for Education Statistics, 1979). Although the programs of some of these institutions are identical in all respects to those of private independent colleges, at many, the religious orientation permeates the institution's academic and administrative life. These institutions range from seminaries to research universities and include such diverse forms as the University of Notre Dame, Wittenberg University, and Beth Medrash Govoha. Their distinctive characteristics were reported by Greeley (1969), Pace (1972), Jencks and Riesman (1977), Hobbs and Meeth (1980), and the National Congress on Church-Related Colleges and Universities (1980). Although many of these institutions enroll a diverse student body, some have strict doctrinal orientations that filter out all students outside the faith, and others impose religious tests upon both students and faculty.

Although institutions do not use socioeconomic status (SES) as a criterion for differentiating students in a strict sense, there are significant SES differences among students at various institutions (often a by-product of high tuition charges and/or a tradition of serving the needs of students of a certain social class) and between institutional types. For example, 1979 data (Astin, King, and Richardson, 1979) showed that compared to freshmen at public two-year colleges, freshmen at private universities were more likely to come from families with incomes over $50 thousand (22 versus 5 percent), less likely to come from families with incomes under $15 thousand (17 versus 38 percent), less likely to have a father who was a semiskilled worker, laborer, or unemployed (6 versus 15 percent), and more likely to have a father who had graduated from college (60 versus 26 percent).

The academic ability of students in colleges and universities varies widely among institutions and between institutional types. Academic ability is usually measured by achievement and aptitude scores on standardized examinations like the Scholastic Aptitude Test, by high school grades or rank in class, or by both factors. Institutions range from those with essentially open-door policies that guarantee admission to all high school graduates (as well as nongraduates over the age of twenty-one), for example, the public community colleges of California, to institutions so selective that fewer than a fraction of 1 percent of the high school graduating class of the nation can meet the admissions criteria, for example, the California Institute of Technology. Other critical institutional factors are related to selectivity, including quality of faculty as evaluated through traditional measures, and availability of educational resources. In general, educational outcomes are related to the qualifications of the entering student, regardless of the resources the institution makes available.

The distribution of institutions by selectivity is quite uneven. Among the 2,700 colleges and universities included in the data bank of the Cooperative Institutional Research Program in 1979, only 307 (11 percent) were identified as having very high or high selectivity and an additional 13 percent (357) as having medium selectivity (Astin, King, and Richardson, 1979).

As with the other sources of constituential differentiation, the geographical constituency of institutions varies significantly. At one extreme are community colleges whose students come exclusively from a small geographical area coterminus with the boundaries of the local school district; at the other extreme are major research universities whose students are drawn from a national and even international pool. Small, nonselective, special-interest private institutions are likely to draw their students from a primarily local constituency (Astin and Lee, 1972); regional state colleges and universities are likely to have all but a small fraction of their students drawn from one state (Dunham, 1969; Harcleroad, Molen, and Van Ort, 1976). In some cases, an institution's geographical constituency may be bifurcated, with undergraduates drawn from an essentially statewide pool, and graduate students drawn from a national pool, as in the case of many land-grant universities (Anderson, 1976).

In addition to these major differences in constituential diversity, other factors distinguish between institutions, related to the distribution of students identified by certain characteristics. For example, institutions differ in the proportion of students residing on campus. In most cases, these differences may not be educationally or administratively significant. At some point, however, as the proportion of residential students increases, the nature of the campus may change from one of narrow scope and part-time commitments to a pervasive community of broad scope and shared norms. Similarly, the mix between graduate and undergraduate students, full- and part-time students, and male and female students at the extremes of the range may be an important source of institutional diversity.

There are also institutions that offer programs meeting the unusual needs of unique populations of students, such as Gaulladet College, which serves the deaf.

Reputational Diversity

In his classic essay, Riesman (1956) described American colleges and universities as forming a snakelike academic procession, in which institutions at the head are models for those that follow. Riesman also commented that because of the complexity of the higher educational system, in this country there is no longer a single prestige system that dominates the various subsystems and institutional types previously described. Even though reputational diversity exists, therefore, it is often difficult to define precisely the factors upon which reputation is based or to identify clearly the groups for which these factors are salient (Kuh, 1981).

Generally, however, a national reputation appears to be related to such factors as undergraduate selectivity (Astin and Henson, 1977; Astin and Solomon, 1979) and the quality of graduate programs as evaluated by peers (Cartter, 1966; Roose and Andersen, 1970; Blau and Margulies, 1974–1975; Cartter and Solomon, 1977). Regional or local reputation may be based as much upon history, notoriety, an outspoken president, or an extensive outreach program as it is upon more traditional standards of academic quality. There are no data that speak to the distribution of prestige among institutions of higher education, but it is reasonable to believe that a majority of institutions in this country are unknown outside a fifty-mile radius of the campus, and only a relatively small number (perhaps less than 100) have names the general public recognizes.

Values and Climate Diversity

The values of institutional constituencies and the consequent campus climate compose another and, in many ways, a more ephemeral source of diversity. During the past fifteen years, there have been several major attempts to analyze and categorize institutional "climates" or "cultures." Studies have indicated significant differences of environments and images among colleges that appear similar in other respects as well as between groups of colleges with differing structures, sizes, or mission (Astin, 1968). The Environmental Assessment Technique (EAT) developed by Astin and Holland (1961) uses size, average intelligence, and the distribution of students by major area of study to develop profiles of institutional environments.

The College and University Environmental Scales (CUES) developed by Pace (1969) contain five dimensions of campus environments (practicality, community, awareness, propriety, and scholarship) that discriminate the cultures of both individual and groups of campuses (Pace, 1974). Similarly, the Clark-Trow typology of college students (Trow, 1962) proposes four student orientations—collegiate, academic, vocational, and nonconformist—that not only define student subcultures on a campus but can indicate a dominant orientation to the entire campus.

Each measure of differential climates or cultures, as well as many others that have been developed (see Baird, Hartnett, and associates, 1980), suggests that many campuses differ significantly in their climates. Although the differences appear quite real and have been found repeatedly in many research programs, it is not clear how large a difference must be before it can be said to represent a significant contribution to institutional diversity. At one extreme may be a small number of institutions whose distinctiveness is reflected in the development of an organizational saga or legend (Clark, 1970); at the other extreme may be many institutions whose climates are, for all practical purposes, indistinguishable one from the other.

Structural Diversity

The final factor related to institutional diversity is the structure(s) of the various institutions within the system. At least two structural elements can be identified: those relating to the external environment of the college and those based upon internal factors.

The two major issues relating to the external structure of institutions are the degree to which they are subject to legal authority beyond their own board of control and whether they exist as a single unit or as an integrated part of a multicampus system. Almost every state now has some means through which it coordinates the activities of some or all of the higher educational institutions within its geographical boundaries. The governing or coordinating boards that perform these functions (generically referred to as "superboards") exercise their authority in differing degrees upon differing categories of institution, depending upon legislation, precedence, and related factors in each state. Not all institutions in a state are subject to the superboard's authority. In some states, one or more public institutions may have been established constitutionally rather than through legislation and are therefore immune from attempts to control by other branches of state government (although obviously not immune from influence). In other states, certain categories of public institutions may be outside the purview of the superboard and able to function relatively autonomously. In many more states, nonpublic institutions may participate voluntarily, or not at all, in attempts to coordinate college activities and programs, either (as in Wisconsin) because there is no statutory authority for any governmental agency to supervise their activities or (as in New Jersey) because several private institutions existed prior to the establishment of legislation conferring rights of program approval on a coordinating board and therefore are considered exempt from its provisions.

In addition to being subject to external legal authority, public institutions particularly (and several private ones as well) are often structured as units of a multicampus system, not having their own board of control but being under the authority of a single board that may have jurisdiction over as many as fifty or more different institutions. Being subject to or immune from the oversight of a state superboard and being a stand-alone institution or part of a multicampus system are two factors that may significantly affect many other areas of institutional functioning, ranging from admissions and graduation requirements to budget control and capital-facilities approval.

Regardless of the differentiation of institutions based upon these external structural factors, there may be differentiation internally. The major internal factor contributing to institutional diversity is the degree to which the internal components of the institution are autonomous within the larger structure. Although most institutions operate with a unitary structure, several have established "cluster colleges"—semiautonomous and relatively self-contained subunits—that in many respects operate as if they were independent of the academic and/or administrative requirements of the parent campus. Examples of this type of structure include the cluster colleges at the University of California, Santa Cruz, and, until recently, the federated college system at Rutgers. Other internal structural differences include the presence or absence of traditional departments (Grant and Riesman, 1978) or, in a small and decreasing number of cases, the absence of the freshman and sophomore years in an upper-division college (Altman, 1970; Bell, 1981).

Summary

This chapter presented an inventory of dimensions in which individual institutions may differ. Programmatic, procedural, systemic, constituential, reputational, and structural variations present a bewildering number of possible combinations. Is the system already so diverse that the present array of institutions can accommodate future needs?

There are two reasons why the probable answer to this question is "no." From an evolutionary perspective, it may appear that since the present system has evolved in response to the demands of the environment and is therefore likely to be the most "fit," efforts should be made to retain it. But as Campbell (1975) pointed out, "wisdom produced by any evolutionary system is always wisdom about past worlds, a fittedness to past selective systems. If those worlds have changed, the adaptations may no longer be useful, may have in fact become harmful" (p. 1106). The environments of higher education are changing, and doing so at an increasing rate. There is no particular reason to believe that the institutions that have developed along the dimensions outlined here in fact are those that will be suited to the needs of the future.

The second reason to question the adequacy of the present system based upon a presentation of these dimensions of diversity is that we have no way of determining whether these dimensions are the ones that will be of the greatest significance in future evolution. The variables outlined are those that have occupied the attention of scholars in the field writing from different academic, political, or social perspectives. The number of variables related to an institution's structure or processes is, for all practical purposes, infinite. Those that have been studied were chosen for reasons unrelated to natural selection. They are without question important dimensions. Whether in fact they include within them the critical variations that will ensure population adaptability 50 or 100 years from now is problematic at best and potentially can be determined only retrospectively.

3

Are Colleges Becoming More Alike?

During the past decade, a small number of scholars have turned their attention to the issue of diversity in higher education. Although all agree upon the importance of diversity, they disagree significantly upon whether diversity is in fact increasing or decreasing. To a great extent, their apparent disagreement is caused by the absence of any common definition of diversity. As a consequence, different studies consider differing variables; one should not be surprised to find differing conclusions as well.

This chapter summarizes previous work in this field, as presented by critical analysts and empirical researchers, and identifies the commonalities and differences in their variables, data, and analyses. It also presents a new perspective on diversity, based upon systems theory, and suggests whether increased or decreased diversity should be expected, according to this model.

Any discussion of diversity must immediately comment upon the increasing difficulty of defining the boundaries of the higher education sector. Particularly within the last five years, educational programs presenting material at a level normally associated with collegiate expectations have burgeoned in business and industrial corporations, hospitals, the armed services, social service agencies, and other noncollegiate settings. Enrollments in such programs may be equal to, or may even exceed, enrollments in colleges and universities. Although much of the educational programming going on in such organizations may be more accurately described as training rather than education, this can also be said of a significant proportion of the programming in some colleges. At the other end of the spectrum, some of these organizations have developed programs of such rigor and quality that they have sought, and received, authority from appropriate state jurisdictions to award degrees.

Any comments concerning diversity must therefore specify whether the concern focuses upon this country's total postsecondary system or the more limited area of the higher education portion. Either focus is subject to criticism. Looking at the entire postsecondary sector certainly gives a more complete view of the totality of alternatives available to potential students, eliminates what may be seen by some as essentially arbitrary and invidious distinctions, and significantly expands the potential diversity in the system. This view also has significant problems because there are no data for making meaningful comparisons with earlier time periods, no definitions that clearly identify whether certain programs are truly postsecondary in nature, no nationally recognized agencies that can speak authoritatively to such matters, and no criteria that would permit a determination of what, if anything, was uniquely "higher" about higher education.

On the other hand, restricting consideration to institutions of higher education and excluding all noncollegiate postsecondary organizations permit analysis of a population of institutions whose composition has been traditionally understood, with an accepted and increasingly sophisticated data base permitting comparisons over extended time periods and with criteria for inclusion defined by authoritative state, regional, and federal agencies. Clarity in definition and precision in analysis are gained, but the cost is exclusion of a large and rapidly growing group of programs from consideration, many of whose offerings are indistinguishable, except on the most formal procedural grounds, from those of colleges and universities.

Recognizing the consequences of doing so, this study restricts its attention solely to institutions of higher education, which are defined as offering "programs terminating in an associate, baccalaureate, or higher degree" (National Center for Education Statistics, 1980a, p. 312). As seen later in this study, even this apparently precise definition contains ambiguities that must be resolved before analysis is possible.

The Critical Analysts

Scholars referred to as critical analysts have considered the issue of diversity in higher education from holistic perspectives and within a social context. They draw their data from both their experiences and those of others, and their qualitative and deductive approach often leads to intellectually powerful and politically influential generalizations.

Riesman issued one of the first and most important statements concerning diversity in post–World War II America. His famous essay "The Academic Procession," first presented in 1956 (Riesman, 1956), metaphorically described the higher education system as a snakelike procession, with a small group of prestigious institutions at its head, a larger group of institutions in the middle attempting to emulate the avant-garde, and a group of academic stragglers in a torporous tail. Riesman recognized that even at the time of his writing (there were 2,008 institutions of higher education and branches in 1959–1960, National Center for Education Statistics, 1980b, p. 102), the system had become so complex that "no single prestige system can dominate the great variety of subsystems" (p. 13). At the same time, he raised the problem of what he referred to as "institutional homogenization" (p. 1), related to the increasing tendency for institutions to follow national rather than regional models, and suggested that educational fashions spread as institutions modeled their behaviors upon those higher than they in the procession.

These concepts were developed more fully in 1968 by

Jencks and Riesman in their important and controversial volume *The Academic Revolution* (1977). The revolution they described was the professoriate's rise to power based upon increased professionalism, reliance upon meritocratic values, and the rise of the university college (that is, the undergraduate college of the research university) as the basic model that all other four-year institutions seek to emulate. As a consequence, the reference groups of colleges changed, moving away from the special interests upon which they were founded toward norms of achievement, competence, and judgment that typify the academic values of national institutions. As these institutions become more alike in their values, their faculties, and the processes by which they select their clientele, commented Jencks and Riesman, "the result is convergence of aims, methods, and probably results" (p. 26).

Jencks and Riesman examined the effects of the academic revolution and found that an increasing adherence to national norms, although creating problems that should be addressed, was a positive and progressive step for American higher education. Newman's *Report on Higher Education* considered the same phenomenon three years later in 1971 and was considerably more disturbing. The thesis of this report, prepared at the request of the secretary of the Department of Health, Education and Welfare, was: "As we have examined the growth of higher education in the postwar period, we have seen disturbing trends towards uniformity in our institutions, growing bureaucracy, overemphasis on academic credentials, isolation of students and faculty from the world—a growing rigidity and uniformity of structure that makes higher education reflect less and less the interests of society" (p. vii).

The report argued that although American higher education appeared to be diverse, it was in fact being increasingly homogenized. By adopting the same methods of teaching and learning and accepting a common educational mission, institutions had become quite similar, and the traditional sources of differentiation among them were fast disappearing. The report noted that the liberal arts curriculum had become the standard, so that specialized institutions such as agricultural or teacher's colleges had become comprehensive colleges and universities. "At the same time that diversity among institutions has declined, diversity in course offerings within each institution has been increasing. Technical colleges have added the humanities; social science departments have been established; traditional disciplines have been subdivided. The uniform acceptance of a diverse curriculum is an indicator of a growing similarity of mission: that of providing general academic education. The system of higher education as a whole is now strikingly uniform: almost all the institutions have the same general image of what they want themselves—and their students—to be" (p. 13).

Each of these three essays considered to varying degrees the growing tensions in the educational system between local and cosmopolitan emphases, and each saw the system as a whole becoming more uniform. For Riesman, the cause was institutional emulation; for Jencks and Riesman, the major factor was the academic revolution; and for Newman, the principal reason was the domination of a single academic mode of teaching and learning. All three factors are of course related to each other, and all three authors might subscribe to the general sense, if not the rhetorical flourish, of Newman's (1971) comment that "the modern academic university has, like a magnet, drawn all institutions towards its organizational form, until today the same teaching method, the same organization by disciplines, and the same academic training for faculty are nearly universal" (p. ix).

More recent considerations of diversity acknowledge the forces seen by earlier analysts but tend to focus more upon factors that continue to differentiate institutions rather than those that at the same time may be making them more uniform. Trow (1979) recognized that diversity is a unique feature of American higher education and that it is currently being threatened by forces toward homogenization and centralization. At the same time, however, he argued that diversity has actually increased with the growth of the system. Among the growth-related components of diversity, he listed the range of studies, services, types of students, forms of institutional organization, modes of governance, and sources of support—a list of factors in some ways broader than those explicitly cited by other authors and thus perhaps in some way accounting for the differences in findings.

In its final report, *Three Thousand Futures: The Next Twenty Years for Higher Education* (1980), the Carnegie Council expressed its concern over the issue of diversity and related in large measure the decline of distinctive colleges to the shifting emphasis from small to large institutions. Acknowledging the recent developing of some new institutions, including those that serve minority groups, those that provide certification rather than instructional service, and those that exist as adjuncts to business firms, the council still believed that proportionately more students were in the same kinds of environments than in the past. The council stated that "The diversity of American higher education used to be found between and among institutions with conformity within each of them; now diversity is more often found within institutions, with the institutions in their entirety being more alike. Fewer institutions have their own strong individual personalities" (p. 22).

Stadtman (1980) most recently considered diversity in the tradition of the critical analysts. He argued that in the past, there was too much emphasis upon the effect of emulation upon diversity. He found that the prevailing changes during the 1970s were not toward university status but toward comprehensiveness. Drawing upon data collected by the Carnegie Council and the National Center for Education Statistics, Stadtman identified a reduction in the number of private colleges and the proportion of students enrolled in private colleges, loss of single-sex institutions, growth of comprehensive institutions, and the closing of small, private colleges. However, he still found that "diversity remains one of the most distinctive and valuable features of American higher education. Predictions of its imminent demise are both premature and overdrawn. Much of the diversity among institutions that has been lost in recent years has been offset by increasing diversity of programs within institutions as they become larger and more comprehensible" (p. 117).

On the one hand, Stadtman's statements could be read as

suggesting that the level of diversity in American higher education has remained unchanged. On the other hand, he arrived at that conclusion by adding negative changes in institutional diversity to positive changes in internal diversity—two factors that, as has been argued already, are not summative because they are negatively correlated.

Without exception, the work of the critical analysts is thoughtful, provocative, and insightful. In sum, they appear to suggest that although institutional diversity may have decreased somewhat over the past twenty years, the system's diversity is still at a high level. Threats of centralization and excessive external control still exist and must be rejected, but the gloomy predictions of only a decade ago do not appear to have been realized. At the same time, it is unclear whether more recent assessments differ from previous ones because of historical changes during the period, differences in the perceptions of the analysts, or differences in the definitions of diversity that, for the critical analysts, for the most part remains a general notion rather than an explicit and measurable variable.

The Empirical Researchers

Over the past decade or so, a number of research efforts have collected and analyzed data that either explicitly or implicitly are related to the question of diversity in higher education. The empirical approach has been useful because it has required scholars to specify the variables under study (thus correcting a weakness of the critical analysts), to develop procedures for collecting and analyzing the data that are consistent with accepted research practice and replicable, and to specify the objective evidence upon which they base their conclusions. Since there is no commonly accepted meaning of "diversity," however, there is also no commonly accepted understanding of which variables are important. For that reason, by and large the studies consider different variables and often exclude large portions of the higher education system, making comparisons between them virtually impossible and trend analysis exceptionally difficult. Most of the studies compiled a large data base, but the number of variables considered was limited, particularly for those studies for which diversity was a secondary rather than primary issue.

Martin (1969) began his study of eight institutions with a belief that the higher education system was characterized by a great diversity of form and function as reflected in differences in size, programs, sources of funding, and structural arrangements. The purpose of his study was to select colleges that differed among these variables, to determine whether they in turn were related to differences in educational goals, assumptions, and values. Although Martin believed that these latter matters were in fact quite uniform, he presumed that a diversity of means would eventually lead to a diversity in ends. This belief in the development of substantive diversity was bolstered by the sense that the unrest of the late 1960s and its new emphasis upon institutional and individual identity had replaced the past concern for institutional imitation.

Data for this study were collected through campus visits, interviews, and questionnaire responses by faculty, students, and administrators. The data did not support the hypotheses.

> Beneath diverse structures and functions we found uniformity in educational assumptions and sociopolitical values across major interest groups and in various types of institutions. This general conclusion will be emphasized throughout this chapter because of its far-reaching significance. American higher education has been characterized by conformity where diversity is needed, that is, at the level of values. External variety and surface change have concealed the conformity and rigidity in fundamental values even as false confidence that differences in external forms and appearances must result in varied internal assumptions, or, from another theoretical perspective, that differences in structure and function are always manifestations of differences in values, have diverted attention from that prerequisite to significant change—examination of the deep values [Martin, 1969, pp. 210–211].

Although Martin did not comment specifically upon the extent to which the form and function of higher education had been changing, he did assume that the system was still characterized by significant diversity. This assumption was itself challenged by Hodgkinson (1971), writing only two years later. Based upon a comparison of 1966 federal data with similar data collected from seventeen to ten years earlier and from responses to questionnaires in which institutional presidents were asked to identify changes for the period 1958–1968, Hodgkinson found the level of institutional diversity in the country decreasing. Institutions increasingly were offering higher degrees and were becoming public, nondenominational, larger, coeducational, multipurposed, and in these and other ways more homogeneous. The study's final conclusion was that "taken as a whole, the amount of institutional diversity in American higher education is decreasing. This is due partially to the pervasive existence of a single status system in higher education, based on the prestigious university offering many graduate programs and preoccupied with research. There are few alternative models to this system now functioning" (p. xv).

Pace's study of diversity (1974) differed from previous research in its methodological rigor, although it focused upon outcomes, as did Martin, and change over time, as did Hodgkinson. Pace's title, *The Demise of Diversity? A Comparative Profile of Eight Types of Institutions,* reflected both his appreciation of the arguments that Martin and Hodgkinson had presented and the somewhat equivocal nature of his findings. His study was based upon the use of the College and University Environmental Scales (CUES), a standardized instrument he developed for measuring perception of college environments on five dimensions: scholarship, awareness, community, propriety, and practicality. Based upon these differential profiles, Pace established eight types of college environments: three liberal arts college types (selective, denominational, and general), three university types (highly selective, less comprehensive, and general comprehensive), and two "other" types related to program (teacher education or technical). CUES was administered to respondents from sixty-seven institutions selected to represent types. The study did not consider whether the distribution of these institutional types had changed over the period but whether the responses of previous graduates (the class of 1950) differed from the responses from the class of 1970. Pace was concerned about whether the groups' college experiences would differ between institutional types and whether "such institutional differences today (class of 1970) were larger or smaller than previously (class of 1950). In other words, "is there now more distinctiveness between institutional types (diversity in the system), or less?" (p. 22).

Contrary to Martin's findings, Pace's data indicated significant differences in the outcomes of different types of institutions, although the data did not indicate whether this was caused by different institutional climates, different kinds of students, or some other factor. Examining a number of variables related to diversity, Pace found institutions less diverse on some measures and more diverse on others over the twenty-year period. His conclusions appear contradictory. On one hand, "There has been some reduction of diversity in the college environment and nature of the college experience, but the diversity of outcomes has been maintained" (p. 127). On the other hand, "about the same level of diversity still exists in the system despite some loss of distinctiveness in certain types of institutions. The case for arguing that there has been a general decline in diversity and distinctiveness does not on the surface appear to be strongly convincing" (p. 130).

Subsequent research on forty private colleges (Anderson, 1977) supported Pace's contention that distinctiveness was being diminished in certain types of institutions. Analyzing changes in CUES scores over a ten-year period, Anderson found adverse environmental changes in colleges that previously had been single-sex or religiously oriented (or both) and that had broadened their mission to become independent or coeducational. In general, these changes tended to move institutions that had been unusually high on some of the CUES scales (thus evidencing a unique educational environment) toward the national means on these scales. Although the sample was not random, and it was too small to assess national trends, the conclusions were thought-provoking. "As more private colleges seek to expand their applicant pool by broadening their missions (single-sex to coeducational, religiously oriented to secular education, the inclusion of career education with liberal arts, an education for the academically disinclined as well as the gifted, and an education for the mature adult as well as the young adult), one can anticipate a further demise of diversity with a concomitant erosion of distinctive educational environments" (pp. 87-88).

Two major studies by Gross and Grambsch (1968, 1974) focused upon universities' institutional goals. Although the study was not concerned primarily with diversity as an issue, the data provided evidence concerning differences in goals of universities with different characteristics as well as changes occurring in such institutions over a relatively brief period. The results appear to contradict those of previous empiricists. Analyzing the responses of 4,500 persons in sixty-eight universities, Gross and Grambsch (1974) found that not only were universities contrasted sharply from other types of institutions, they were different from each other and growing more distinctive and diverse over time. "There are—and this is our most important finding—distinct signs that universities are more sharply differentiated than they were in 1964, so that it seems increasingly inappropriate to think of 'university' as a uniform category of analysis. . . . Our evidence is that universities are dividing into noncompeting clusters, each cluster beginning to define its own area in its own way" (p. 117).

The argument for increasing diversity is further supported by the work of Baldridge and others (1978), which used questionnaire data from a sample of over 4,000 persons at 249 colleges and universities. The purpose of the study was to assess the differences in patterns of management and governance, professional autonomy, institutional climate, and other organizational factors related to institutions divided into a typology of eight types. The types themselves were developed from the Carnegie Council's (1976) classification system. Baldridge concluded that "In spite of many public pronouncements of growing homogeneity, we still believe that the American higher education system is incredibly diverse, *and growing more so*" [emphasis added] (p. 49). Baldridge recognized that disagreements about assessing levels and changes in diversity among different scholars arose from differences in the variables they considered, but at the same time he did not clearly identify the baseline against which he compared his own variables or present any data to support his contention that diversity is increasing. However, Baldridge did present compelling evidence that colleges and universities in his typology are different in many ways, and he offered the idea that the change from primarily private to primarily public control in higher education may in fact increase rather than decrease diversity. He argued that this is so because public systems can maximize diversity through planning, while private institutions presumably may become more alike through uncontrolled competition. The merits of this concept are discussed at greater length in Chapter Seven; at this point, however, it is an example of the difficulties attendant to single-variable definitions of diversity. Although advocates of private institutions tend to equate diversity with the maintenance of their sector, growth of public institutions and diminution of the private sector conceivably could promote other forms of institutional diversity that might go unnoticed if source of control is the only value examined.

Is Diversity Changing?—A Conceptual Approach

The work of the critical analysts and the empirical researchers can be cited to support claims that diversity in higher education is decreasing, is increasing, or has remained constant. Scholarship of the early 1970s and before tends to endorse findings suggesting diminished diversity; more recent works are more optimistic. Many of these studies present analyses of social, educational, and related factors that supposedly "explain" the findings. This section provides a conceptual framework within which these explanations can be assessed.

The natural selection model, upon which this book is based, argues that the diversity of organizational structures is related to the diversity of the environment with which they interact. If the environment is more uniform and contains a relatively small number of niches, it will be able to support only a small number of different kinds of organizations. If the environment is more diverse, the number of potential niches will increase and the number of different organizational forms that can be supported will increase also. Institutional diversity in higher education is thus directly related to the environment. This relationship can be clarified by considering organizational-environmental relations from an open-systems perspective.

Viewed as an organization, a college or university can be seen as a system (1) composed of a number of subsystems and (2) existing within an environment. Each subsystem interacts with the environment, being influenced by it and in turn having an influence upon it. Each organizational subsystem also influences each other. Figure 1 graphically depicts the relationships between institutional subsystems and the environment.

This organizational system model views organizations as having five major subsystems. These subsystems, and an example of their interdependent relationships to the environment in the case of colleges and universities, are as follows.

Goals and Values Subsystem. Institutions of higher education have many goals and values that have been accepted from the broader socioeconomic environment and that in turn affect that environment. An example is an institution's development of a commitment to social equity and equal educational opportunity in response to changing societal needs and expectations. As this goal and this value become internalized within the organization, they affect students who then graduate and through their participation in the environment continue to alter societal expectations concerning social equity, leading to still further institutional responses.

Technical Subsystem. Colleges and universities accept inputs from the environment in the form of students, faculty, and fiscal resources, and after transforming them in some way, they return them to the environment. The processes, equipment, and facilities by which input is transformed into output are the institution's technology. This might include its use of lectures, seminars, examinations, self-study, television, and the

Figure 1. The Organizational System.
(From F. E. Kast and J. E. Rosenzweig, *Contingency Views of Organizations and Management,* Chicago: Science Research Associates, 1973, p. 14.)

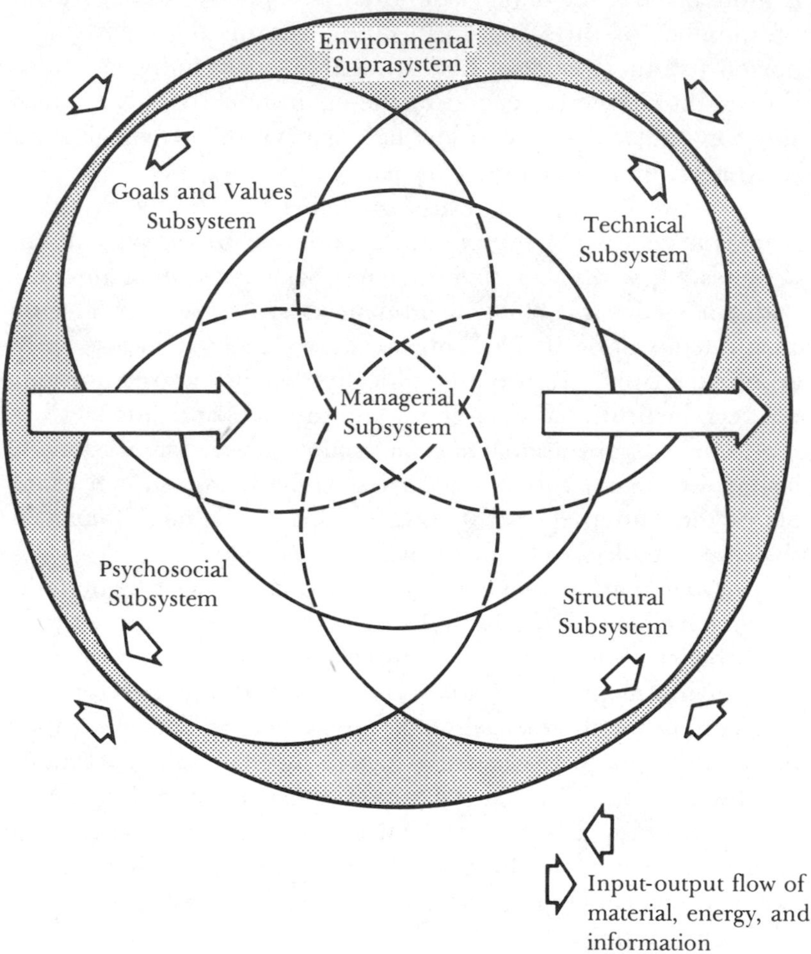

other means by which it characteristically carries out its educational functions. An example of a new technological force in colleges and universities is the microcomputer. As microcomputers increasingly become available, they will change the processes by which education is conducted and thereby change the ongoing technical subsystem. At the same time, the increased use of such technologies will encourage manufacturers to look for new ways in which the machines can be used, thus continuing to change the environment that affects college and university technology.

Structural Subsystem. Colleges and universities have ways by which various tasks are divided and processes through which these activities are coordinated. For example, institutions are usually characterized by the formation of the faculty into academic departments. This structural form encourages specialization and defines for the environment the legitimacy of certain fields. In turn, there are pressures from the environment to authenticate new areas of knowledge by creating still more specialized departments or other academic structures.

Psychosocial Subsystem. As in all other organizations, persons in colleges and universities interact with each other in certain ways, fill certain roles, and have certain expectations as to how influence is to be exercised. These factors are perhaps even more important in educational institutions than others because of these organizations' unusual reliance upon normative rather than utilitarian processes to control behavior. An example of an environmental influence upon the psychosocial subsystem would be an AAUP policy statement concerning the appropriate faculty role in institutional governance. Acceptance of this norm by increasing numbers of faculty would create expectations of role behaviors that in turn would influence the content of future AAUP policy statements.

Managerial Subsystem. The managerial subsystem has the responsibility of coordinating each of the other subsystems as the organization goes about its business of setting goals, directing activities, planning, and performing related functions. The development of an institutional long-range plan, for example, may change the perception that other organizations (such as government or funding agencies) have of a specific college or university and thus encourage or discourage future planning activities.

Each subsystem is related not only to the environment through the flow of materials, energy, and information as inputs and outputs but to each of the other organizational subsystems.

For example, the introduction of microcomputers into the technical subsystem leads to problems and issues related to the other subsystems: psychosocial (how can faculty be encouraged to experiment with the new technology); structural (will a new unit have to be formed to administer the creation of software); goals and values (is the new technology compatible with traditional student-teacher relationships); and managerial (what are the implications of the use of microcomputers for institutional budgeting). The interdependence of the subsystems suggests that any change in any subsystem will have an effect upon all other subsystems. Since these subsystems are loosely coupled (Weick, 1976), the effect may not be direct, may not be immediate, and may not even be visible to casual observation. However, it is clear that "major modification in any one of these subsystems creates waves of interaction and change in other subsystems" (Kast and Rosenzweig, 1973, p. 15).

These concepts can now be related to the issue of institutional diversity. A situation of minimal diversity would be expected to occur when institutions all experienced the same environment and had identical subsystems. In such a case, institutions would have the same goals, have common structures, perform similar tasks with similar technology, share similar processes of group dynamics, and establish the same management processes. Hawley (1968) suggested that, as a general principle of human ecology, "Units subject to the same environmental conditions . . . acquire a similar form of organization. They must submit to standard terms of communication and to standard procedures in consequence of which they develop similar internal arrangements within limits imposed by their respective sizes" (p. 334). Should the environment change, various institutions would be expected to respond to it in quite the same ways. In contrast, there would be maximum diversity when institutions functioned in quite different environments and operated with subsystems as different as possible from each other.

Several critical correlaries can be developed from this orientation. First, in any set of organizations, as the environment interacting with any particular subsystem becomes more similar, that subsystem will become more and more alike within the various organizations. For example, as various kinds of institutions confront a standard regulation concerning accounting procedures for federal funds (an environmental input), these institutions' managerial subsystems will respond by becoming more alike. Similarly, as more and more faculty receive their graduate training from major institutions or from teachers who have studied in major institutions, their sense of what is to be taught and how it is to be taught will become more alike, and the goals and values subsystems of their institutions will become increasingly similar. This process has been accelerated by the increasingly tight academic job market, which as one consequence has led to nonselective institutions appointing new faculty who previously would have worked in prestigious schools.

In the same way, as similar subsystems in different organizations tend to become more alike as they respond to similar environmental pressures, they change the other subsystems within those organizations so that they, too, tend to become more alike. For example, as faculty are increasingly socialized during their training in large, research-oriented institutions, their expectations of their roles in governance when they enter the field will also tend to become more common. The tendency for institutional subsystems to become increasingly similar in response to undifferentiated environmental pressures helps explain apparent institutional anomalies, such as community colleges that require publications for promotion or the development of adult education programs in liberal arts colleges.

If organizational subsystems that are related to diversity tend to become more alike as their environments become more similar, institutional diversity would be expected to increase as institutions encountered increasingly different environmental pressures and decrease as their environments became more similar. Although there are no empirical data that deal extensively with changes in the environments of higher education institutions, it can be argued that in general they are becoming more alike. A natural consequence of this would be that institutional diversity is decreasing.

A number of factors related to the proposed model's subsystems enter into this judgment. For example, institutions are increasingly part of statewide systems (in the public sector) or influenced by the decisions or recommendations of statewide coordinating boards. Although the power of these superboards differs in different jurisdictions, the boards often act to create data banks requiring common definitions, to require program development and review carried out in certain formats, to require development of budgets in prescribed methods, and (in the public sector) to establish a specified administrative structure. Not only do these and other requirements tend to make the management subsystems of institutions under their jurisdictions more and more alike, the state boards themselves are linked through networks, such as Education Commission of the States, National Center for Higher Education Management Systems, and the State Higher Education Executive Officers Association, so that new approaches in one geographical area can become quickly disseminated in others.

Other environmental factors impinging upon colleges' and universities' managerial subsystems include the development of federal legislation and associated agency rules and guidelines imposing uniform procedures for reporting expenditure of federal funds, accounting for faculty time, reporting enrollment and other data, defining satisfactory student progress toward a degree, and other matters; state and federal affirmative action requirements; national associations such as the National Association of College and University Business Officers, which define accepted accounting practice; federal court decisions defining due process for faculty members; and the increasing professionalization of college and university administration, which might be described as the second academic revolution.

Goals and values subsystems have been affected by general acceptance of the role of colleges and universities in developing compensatory educational programs and in other ways responding to issues of social justice (which may also have the effect of increasing the heterogeneity of students among campuses); the movement toward secularization of institutional control and coeducational student bodies; the broadening of institutional missions to be attractive to as many potential applicants as possible; and the success of the academic revolution, which increasingly has made academic and scholarly values the dominant theme of institutions.

As institutions become more secular, larger, and more complex, psychosocial subsystems within them are apt to become more uniform. The orientation of faculty and administrators toward their roles is likely to reflect national rather than local models, normative statements by professional associations become absorbed into the institutional culture, and collective bargaining introduces new psychological forces and expectations as well as national organizations that codify and disseminate them. As participants' training and socialization processes in different kinds of academic organizations become more uniform, their perceptions of the environment become more uniform as well. "The effects of these processes is to homogenize perceptions across organizations and to make each organization less sensitive to the unique characteristics of its local environment. If a local government is benign and has a wide tolerance for deviations from the ideal structure or performance, then socially induced misperceptions are not fatal" (Aldrich and Pfeffer, 1976, p. 95).

External forces affecting the structural subsystem include the development of new positions required by regulations affecting all institutions, such as affirmative action officer; the professionalization of certain roles that then lead to common program structures (particularly true in the student personnel and business areas); expansion of state multicampus systems, which directly or indirectly influence organization structure; and the development of uniform procedural requirements by federal and other agencies, which require the development of specific structures.

Finally, the technology of the academy (that is, the people, processes, and equipment that transform the "input" into "output") is being influenced by the external environment and being made more uniform. Differences in the preparation of faculty, which once typified different kinds of institutions, have been eroded; courses offered through newspapers or television provide a uniform experience in campuses across the country; single-purposed institutions are being developed into multipurpose ones; the one distinctive aspect of a college program (its general education component) is becoming less visible and important; and for the most part, recent experiments with new teaching styles have floundered and been replaced by the traditional reliance upon lecture, recitation, and laboratory.

The picture presented is a bleak one. It is also one-sided, but there is great difficulty in attempting to identify similar forces operating in the contemporary environment that would tend to make institutional subsystems more *different* and therefore institutions themselves more diverse. One such force is the often-heard claim that, at least in centralized state systems, planning and other management controls can establish unique missions and identities for institutions and prevent them from becoming more and more alike as they compete in the marketplace for a dwindling number of students—a concept of "diversity by design." This argument proposes that "a system can achieve greater *diversity* among postsecondary institutions, no matter what the conventional wisdom about the freedom guaranteed by the absence of coordination. A system can assure greater *accountability,* and yet it is also best equipped to assure institutional *autonomy.* A systemwide approach can achieve a greater *richness,* especially through intercampus actions. And [by] a systemwide approach higher education can stimulate greater experimentation and educational change" (Kaplan, 1976, p. xi). But there is no guarantee that an institution planned to be different in a state system can sustain that difference in the face of extreme environmental demands. At Ramapo College, founded in the New Jersey State College System as a nontraditional liberal arts college, for example, business majors composed a large proportion of a recent freshman class. But even if institutions with unique programs and orientations could be founded and supported, from the perspective of evolution that already has been discussed, the concept of diversity by design is a contradiction in terms. Unless it is known in advance which characteristics of an institution in the future may prove to be the ones with the greatest survival value, there is no guarantee that the right combination of attributes would be incorporated into the design. (In fact, if it were possible to accurately predict such things, diversity as it has been defined here would not be such a critical dimension of an educational system.)

Although some of those who considered the issue of diversity in the past disagree, the concepts developed in this chapter support the prediction that diversity in higher education is decreasing. The next chapter considers the issue of defining diversity so that it can be analytically studied.

4

Ways of Measuring Diversity

This study is based upon the natural selection (also known as the population ecology) model, which posits that changes in the population of organizations can be considered analogous to the selective retention processes of biological evolution. Within the context of this model, diversity is seen as the institutional equivalent of "variation," the first element (followed by selection and retention) in the three-stage process essential to evolution. Changes in the distribution of organizational forms are viewed as a response by the system of institutions to more closely "fit" the demands of the social environment. Consistent with this model, this focus is upon the population of organizations rather than individual organizations within the population (Hannan and Freeman, 1977).

Several conditions should obtain to justify the use of the natural selection model. Campbell (1969) argued that if systematic selection is to occur in a social system, numerous organizations must be involved and there must be a high mortality rate. If these factors are not present, "the environment or selective criteria may be too inconsistent, and the number of units too small, for any evolutionary process to take place" (p. 75). These conditions appear to be met by the existence of 3,150 colleges and universities and the rates of institutional failure discussed in Chapter One. The model also requires that organizations be considered over a significant time span (Aldrich and Pfeffer, 1976). Although expanding the time period encompassed by this study—1960 to 1980—would have been highly desirable, the great number of changes that occurred then and their systematic nature suggest that the twenty-year period meets at least the minimal time requirements.

Institutional Types

A model of organizational evolution based upon population biology requires that there must be something equivalent to what biologists refer to as a "species." Although there are no agreed-upon criteria for establishing organizational species, Hannan and Freeman (1977) suggested that organizations can be treated as species by considering that "organizational form is a blueprint for organizational action, for transforming inputs into outputs" (p. 935). That blueprint, in turn, can be determined by examining the organization's formal structure, activities, and normative order. In this view, formal structure can be determined by tables of organization, written rules of operation, and similar artifacts; patterns of activity can be assessed by considering what actually gets done in the organization and who does it; and normative order can be determined by understanding what ways of organizing are considered appropriate by persons in the organization and by external constituencies. Aldrich (1979), considering the same issue, defined organizational form as consisting of "specific configurations of goals, boundaries, and activities" (p. 28).

Once it has been determined what property or properties of organizations will be used to construct the typology, qualitative differences between the organizational forms can be found, and thus populations can be identified. Developing typologies of organizations is not an easy task; and if the number of typologies for organizations found in the literature is any indication, there is no consensus about a typology that could be used to study more than a single aspect of organizations (Scott, 1981). Organizations that belong to a single category under one typology may be classified under two separate categories in another typology. Typologies can be arbitrary; therefore, a caveat for the use of this model is that the method followed for classifying populations could have a biasing effect.

Selecting the factors defining an organizational species is obviously important for many studies since improper classification may influence the findings (Scott, 1981) and distort an attempt to relate any specific characteristics to adaptability. In the absence of empirical data or previous studies that define those aspects of organizational form that would be the most pertinent, this study had to develop its own definition. Since the purpose of this study is to investigate changes in the range of variations rather than the reasons for changes over time, errors in classifying institutions probably have less consequence for this investigation than they might for others.

In this study, institutional species are defined according to six variables. Each variable is commonly used to classify and differentiate colleges and universities, although no previous study considered all the variables in combination. No claim is or can be made that the variables are unquestionably the most appropriate for the purposes of differentiating species. As Aristotle considered men and birds related because each walked on two legs, so these variables may prove at some future and more enlightened time as incorrect as they are intuitively obvious. However, they appear to have "face validity," and the variables selected have other virtues as well: They are visible, are relatively measurable, appear to be related to educational outcomes, and are commonly accepted as reflecting differences in institutional form and function.

Defining institutional types by these six variables is not meant to suggest that all institutions within the same type are identical. It is obvious that in at least some way every institution in this country is different from every other. One can sense an idea of the extent of these differences by a reading of Riesman's (1981) almost encyclopedic descriptions of programs, orientations, and unique features of various institutions. At the same time, there are ways groups of institutions are alike as well, sharing characteristics that define their basic form and structure even though elements of their programs may be different. Following Ehrlich's discussion in Chapter One, these two aspects can be thought of as analogous to species and genetic variability in biology. The basic elements of organizational form and structure that are defined by the six variables used in this study are considered as defining species. The many other differences between institutions of the same type are considered as representing genetic variability and are not further considered in the study. This distinction between two important elements may be incorrect, but at this stage in the consideration of colleges and universities from an ecological perspective, there is no way of absolutely differentiating a species characteristic from an example of genetic variability.

For the purposes of this study, describing institutions with different characteristics as species is methodologically appropriate, but it can be misleading in many ways. Using a term with precise biological definition to identify groups of institutions developed using arguable criteria, and adopting a conceptual orientation that is by no means as accepted by organization theorists as it is by biologists, may cause readers to inappropriately assume (despite disclaimers to the contrary) a degree of precision in measurement and consensus in approach that does not exist. To avoid this error, rather than using the term species, institutions sharing identical values of all six variables are referred to as belonging to the same institutional "type."

Defining the Variables

The six variables used to define institutional type are control, size, sex of students, program, degree level, and minority enrollments. They were selected from among the much larger number of variables related to diversity that were discussed in Chapter Two based on a procedural criterion and two substantive criteria. The procedural criterion was that values of the variable had to be available from existing and available data bases for the sample institutions for both 1960 and 1980 since the scope of the study precluded collecting data directly from individual campuses. This criterion eliminated a number of possible variables from consideration. For example, the distribution of residential and commuting students and the selectivity of the campus and the high school grades and test scores of successful applicants both are obviously dimensions significantly differentiating colleges and universities. These data are available for 1980 (or a year close to that), but they were not for 1960 and therefore could not be considered.

One substantive criterion was that the variable be one visible to the environment and salient to potential constituents who decided whether the institution would be provided with resources. The resources an institution requires are in the form of money, students, political influence, prestige, or other material and nonmaterial inputs. Decisions to provide or withhold these resources are "made" by the environment through the cumulative effects of individual actions taken by potential "supporters"—donors, students, legislators, professional groups, and others. Such decisions cannot be made upon the basis of characteristics that for the most part are not available to the perception of potential resource providers, and they would not be expected to be based upon factors that may be visible but of little or no importance to potential supporters' decision processes. Campus climate, for example, may be an important determinant of student outcomes and a major factor in institutional diversity, but it is generally not visible to potential constituents. On the other hand, the academic calendar is a clearly visible institutional characteristic, but except under unusual circumstances, it would not be considered important enough by constituents to enter into resource-allocation decisions.

The second substantive criterion was that the variables being considered must be related both to important aspects of institutional organization and form and to either student learning and development or major institutional activities and processes. Different variables were assessed against this criterion by reviewing the work of scholars in the field.

Following is a discussion of the variables finally selected, their possible values, and a summary of the existing evidence supporting their impact upon student learning or organizational functioning.

Control (Four Values). Institutional control was coded as public, independent, religious, or proprietary. Differences in this variable are related to organizational structure, goals, activities, and outcomes.

Public institutions are usually directly related to other governmental agencies because of common personnel, budgeting, administrative, and similar policies; are subject to varying degrees of influence by statewide higher education boards; and are often part of multicampus state systems. To any great extent, none of these characteristics are true for institutions in the other three categories. Astin's (1977) longitudinal study on the effects of different types of colleges upon students' attitudes, beliefs, self-concepts, behavior patterns, educational attainment, and career development revealed that public institutions, after controlling for other variables, are not as distinctive as either private or religiously affiliated institutions.

Astin found that students at public institutions were dissatisfied with classroom instruction, and students in public universities perceived that their institutions placed too much emphasis upon social life. Based upon his findings, Astin (1977) concluded that "the only areas where public institutions provide greater satisfaction are the variety of courses offered and the emphasis on social life" (p. 244). Because they are not restricted by state controls, private institutions are believed to have greater freedom to model their curriculum after a particular philosophical orientation (Keeton, 1971); to develop special programs and to have a special purpose (El-Khawas, 1976); and to be innovative (Riesman, 1981).

Although nonselective private colleges resemble public colleges in several dimensions, students at private colleges have more personal contact with their instructors, while students at public campuses perceive their environment as cold and impersonal (Astin and Lee, 1972). Attending a private institution has positive effects upon student self-concept and artistic interests, student-faculty interaction and familiarity with faculty in one's major field, involvement in student government and leadership development, and satisfaction with the institution's academic reputation and classroom instruction (Astin, 1977). Many of the positive findings associated with private colleges are attributed to such schools being more homogeneous, smaller, and residential and to their emphasis upon undergraduate teaching. In addition, some schools have established images—nationally or locally—that in turn attract students "familiar with the image and favorably disposed to it" (Feldman and Newcomb, 1969, p. 331). Evidence shows that the goals of many public and private institutions are considerably different. A major study of public and private universities, for example, indicated that of forty-seven possible goals, public and private university faculty and administrations agreed upon only three of the top ten (Gross and Grambsch, 1974).

Religiously affiliated colleges are far from being a homogeneous group. Under the general umbrella of Catholic and Protestant colleges, differences exist according to the founding order or denomination with which they are associated. Differences also exist because of factors of selectivity, size, and geographical location. The most important difference, however, seems to depend upon the strength of the religious affiliation. Colleges at which the legal and spiritual ties are stronger have a greater sense of community and are more likely to have distinctive environments (Pace, 1972; Anderson, 1977). Studies and reports by Astin (1975, 1977), Riesman (1981), and Keeton (1971) indicated that institutions under religious control instill altruistic values, increase student-faculty relations, reduce the chance of dropping out, and offer students an opportunity to be in an environment in which peers and teachers are likely to share similar values and beliefs.

Proprietary institutions offer an "alternative channel" into postsecondary education for those students whose vocational needs have not been met by either high school or programs offered at local community colleges (Trivett, 1974). Proprietary schools are believed to be particularly adept at meeting students' vocational needs because they use teaching techniques different from those practiced in academically oriented institutions, instructors have extensive practical experience, courses last a shorter period, and scheduling is flexible (Worthington, 1973, cited in Trivett, 1974, p. 7). Proprietary schools survive because they restrict themselves to providing job-related training aimed at full-time placement in the shortest possible time (Erickson and others, 1972, cited in Trivett, 1974, p. 16) rather than attempting to embrace a variety of purposes, as community colleges do. And unlike community colleges, their dropout rates are low (Belitsky, 1970, cited in Trivett, 1974, p. 33).

Curriculum (Four Values). The four values that were assigned to an institution's curriculum were liberal arts (institutions whose programs were primarily in the arts and sciences, with little if any attention to professional preparation); comprehensive (programs in both liberal arts and professional and technical areas); professional/technical (colleges and universities whose programs were focused explicitly upon preparing for a career in a specific profession or technical area, with few if any degree programs in traditional liberal arts areas); and teacher education (an institution primarily concerned with training persons for teaching in elementary and secondary schools). Differences in curriculum have clear implications for organizational structure, the preparation and activities of faculty, the motivation and experiences of students, and organizational norms.

In many cases, the coding of institutions upon this variable was problematic. The definitions and variables the federal government used to describe institutional programs changed considerably during the twenty-year study period. Protocols were developed that attempted to make the definitions between the two study years as comparable as possible, but without detailed reviews of catalogues, enrollment data, and similar material, there is no way of ensuring the complete reliability and comparability of these classifications. Categorizing institutions based upon degrees awarded, for example, would yield different distributions than self-reported directory information. The most significant difficulties arise in attempting to differentiate between comprehensive institutions and those that identify themselves as liberal arts colleges but that also offer programs in business, education, and other professional areas.

Because their specialized or focused orientation permits the development of coherent curriculum and encourages the recruitment and self-selection of students and faculty sharing common values and concerns, institutions that "specialize" in the liberal arts, a technical or professional program, or teacher education can be less highly structured and internally differentiated than comprehensive institutions.

Colleges' curriculum orientations are related to student outcomes. Positive outcomes are associated mostly with colleges that continue to offer a traditional liberal arts curriculum. Not surprisingly, these are also the colleges that have remained small, offer a baccalaureate as their highest degree, and are, for the most part, under private control. A liberal arts curriculum is deemed particularly advantageous for students planning to continue on to graduate work and professional degrees in the traditional learned professions (Clark, 1978; Jencks and Reisman, 1977). Other positive outcomes of liberal arts colleges are cohesiveness and cooperativeness in the peer environment, familiarity with instructors, and concern for the individual student (Astin, 1968).

In the last two decades, colleges have tended to move away from a liberal arts curriculum and to become more comprehensive to make curricular diversity possible. The move toward comprehensiveness, however, has resulted in the growth of institutions and thus changed their character in ways not altogether positive for students (Smith and Bernstein, 1979). Moreover, rather than taking advantage of the many offerings available, students in institutions with a comprehensive curriculum tend to specialize instead (Blackburn and others, 1976; Warren, 1977, cited in Smith and Bernstein, 1979, p. 8).

Teacher's colleges and technological institutions offer students two other types of curricula. Under the pressures of declining enrollments and reduced demand for teachers, teacher's colleges, however, are quickly disappearing. In both the public and private sector, many teacher's colleges have evolved from single- to multipurpose (Dunham, 1969). When teacher's colleges were studied in the 1960s, they did not exhibit environments that were particularly distinctive, they were observed to have a strong orientation toward femininity, and they offered their students a great amount of leisure time. Students were not active participants in the classroom, they did not engage in frequent interaction with instructors, and academic competitiveness was perceived as being very low (Astin, 1968, p. 122). A later study in the 1970s (Astin, 1977) yielded similar findings. Student satisfaction with the intellectual environment, student-faculty relations, satisfaction with the classroom instruction, and variety of course offerings were all negatively affected by teacher's colleges. Technological institutions, on the other hand, were shown "to possess the most unique student bodies and environments" (Astin, 1968, p. 123) when studied in the 1960s. The peer environment of these institutions scored high in competitiveness and degree of independence and low in social life, femininity, and cultural activities (Astin, 1968, p. 123). More recently, however, students at technological institutions were found to be the most dissatisfied with the overall institution (Astin, 1977).

Some of the negative consequences associated with these two types of specialized colleges may be related more to factors such as student composition and selectivity rather than the quality, depth, and breadth of the curriculum.

Institutional Size (Three Values). Institutions in the sample were categorized as small (under 1,000 headcount enrollment), medium (1,000 to 2,500), or large (2,501 and higher). A large body of evidence indicates that size is related to institutional activities, structure, goals, and normative order and thus is defensible as a variable for differentiating between institutional types.

Regarding structure, larger institutions are more complex, more differentiated, more impersonal, and have more levels of administration than smaller ones; the differences are so significant that Blau (1973) said "the size of an academic institution unquestionably has a predominant effect on its character" (p. 252). Increasing size also increases the development of specialization, decreases faculty commitment to the institution, increases faculty autonomy, and changes the activities in which faculty participate (Baldridge and others, 1978).

A long tradition of research and analysis (Feldman and Newcomb, 1969; Astin, 1977; Pace, 1979; Smith and Bernstein, 1979; Astin, 1968; Chickering, 1969, Riesman, 1981; Bowen, 1977; Barker and Gump, 1964) consistently supports the existence of strong relationships between institutional size and other variables relating to activities, goals, campus climate, and student outcomes. Smaller campuses are more likely to have a coherent and distinctive climate; their students are more likely to be actively involved in campus activities, to enjoy closer relationships with faculty, and to undergo greater changes in the development of values and a sense of responsibility than students at larger campuses. The overall positive impact of small colleges upon student development has been attributed to environmental qualities in these institutions that contribute to a feeling of community, cohesiveness, shared educational and social experiences, and, most important, a concern for the individual. The recurrent theme in the research findings is that size has an important bearing upon students' sense of unity and identification with their institution.

There are two major questions about the use of size as a dimension of institutional type. First, in view of institutions' propensity to increase in size, what is the justification for considering that a college that, for example, has grown from an enrollment of 2,000 to 4,000 is now of a different institutional type? Are such changes more supportive of a resource dependence model or a natural selection one? These are difficult questions to answer. The use of size is justified because increased size is related to important changes in structure, complexity, and climate. At some point, there has to be a judgment that the qualitative and quantitative differences are significant enough to justify placing institutions in different categories. Because of the changes in communications patterns, interpersonal relationships, administrative structure, and related factors that accompany size, it also seems appropriate to consider a large institution not just as a "grown-up" small one but as a different type altogether. Considerations of the growth of other organizations have reached this same conclusion. "If it is true that organizational form changes with size, selection mechanisms may indeed operate with regard to the size distribution. When big organizations prevail it may be useful to view this as a special case of selection, in which the movement from 'small form' is theoretically indistinguishable from the dissolution ('death') of small organizations and their replacement by (the 'birth' of) large organizations" (Hannan and Freeman, 1977, p. 938).

Second, what is the justification for the choice of the three values of size used in this study? The three values are admittedly arguable. The group of 1,000 and under students was determined as the limit within which much campus communication could take place through interpersonal interaction in small groups and a vigorous and forceful student culture could exist (Chickering, 1969). It was also the level that has been suggested as the point below which economies of scale cannot be maintained and at which the risk of being unable to provide an intellectually challenging environment for students in a liberal arts college exists (Carnegie Commission, 1971b).

The opportunities for campus intimacy appear to disappear above the 1,000-student level, but a larger campus could still function reasonably informally and without a great deal of differentiation and specialization. The boundary of this possibility was placed at 2,500 students, a number further justified by the Carnegie Commission's (1971b) recommendations that this was approximately the minimal level for effective operation of a two-year institution and the maximum level for a sound liberal arts college.

As institutions become larger than 2,500 students, their structures, programs, and climate are likely to change still further. Although clearly there are significant quantitative and qualitative differences between a campus of 2,500 and one of 25,000 students, the small number of very large campuses in 1960, the lack of any recognized basis for differentiating between them, and the desire to keep the number of values of variables to a minimum so that the number of institutional types not be unduly inflated all led to the decision to treat all institutions over 2,500 in a single category.

Degree Level (Four Values). Institutions in the sample were identified upon the basis of the highest degree offered.

The values included two-year institutions, baccalaureate institutions, institutions offering master's degrees, and those offering doctor's degrees. Much evidence indicates that the goals, faculty and student activities, and normative values of institutions offering degrees at these levels are different enough to consider them related to institutional type.

Two-year colleges, four-year institutions, and graduate-level universities differ as to the programs they offer; faculty's professional tasks, relationship to their environment, size, and complexity; governance and management processes; levels of faculty preparation and faculty influence; and similar measures of organizational structure and functioning (Baldridge and others, 1978).

The institutions have different goals as well. Community colleges provide access, remedial education, and comprehensive programs meeting local community needs as well as extensive nondegree programming to a nonselective student body. Four-year institutions serve clienteles ranging from nonselective to highly selective, emphasize teaching the undergraduate, and offer both traditional liberal arts degrees and more recently developed professional and technical programs. The ability to award master's degrees often implies a greater commitment to professional education than that found in many four-year institutions, and it is often seen in institutions serving regional rather than local needs. Institutions offering doctor's degrees give greater attention to research and scholarship than do the other schools.

Research indicates significant differences in the impact of these categories of institutions upon students. Astin (1977), for example, produced evidence that attending a two-year college—whether public or private—does not have the same effect upon students as do four-year colleges and universities. Students at two-year schools are less likely to become involved in student government, participate in athletics, be outspoken in the classroom, be on familiar terms with faculty in their major fields, and attain leadership positions (Astin, 1977). Among the most alarming consequences of attending a two-year college are that it reduces one's chances of implementing career plans in almost every field (Astin, 1977) and the chance of completing a liberal arts degree (Breneman and Nelson, 1981).

Four-year colleges provide distinctive environments; they have been found to yield positive outcomes for most of the dimensions considered as making college-going a meaningful experience in the course of a person's lifetime: student-faculty interaction, familiarity with faculty in the major field, outspokenness in the classroom, involvement in student government, and athletic involvement (Astin, 1977).

In this study, institutions offering master's degrees were coded separately from those offering doctor's degrees. However, since the literature discusses the general effect of graduate work upon undergraduate education, both types of institutions are mentioned here together. The most common observation about institutions that offer graduate-level degrees and emphasize research is that the instruction and intellectual development of graduate students take precedence over the general education of the undergraduates (Feldman and Newcomb, 1969). Gaff (1973) concluded that "the large, research oriented, graduate institutions . . . less often fostered the conditions which were found to be associated with a liberal education of undergraduates" (p. 620). Due to their emphasis on specialized education, universities may be unable to provide experiences undergraduates associate with increased satisfaction with college attendance; for example, student-faculty interaction, concern for the individual, and involvement in research projects.

From the research findings reviewed, the traditional four-year college, with its emphasis upon undergraduate teaching, the development of the whole person, and general collegiate atmosphere, apparently continues to have more positive impact upon students' academic and social development than do either two-year colleges or universities.

Sex (Two Values). Institutions were categorized as either coeducational or single-sex. Because of the relatively small number of institutions involved and the desire to limit the number of possible institutional types, colleges for men only and for women only were treated as having identical values on this variable. The argument for doing so is similar to that justifying combining Catholic, Protestant, Jewish, and other nonsecular institutions under the heading "religious control."

The major effects of the sex variable are upon organizational activities and the normative order of the institutions. Anderson (1977), Jencks and Riesman (1977), and Gappa and Uehling (1979), among others, noted differences in the climate and activities of single-sex institutions. Astin (1977) conducted the most extensive comparison of the differences between coeducational and single-sex campuses, based upon extensive empirical data. His findings indicated that both men's and women's colleges, compared to coeducational ones, increase student involvement in academics, increase interaction with faculty, and lead to increased personal self-esteem. Women in women's colleges are also more likely to attain positions of leadership, participate in student government, develop high aspirations, and graduate. Men in men's colleges do better academically and are more likely to participate in athletics and honors programs. In both men's and women's colleges, students are more satisfied with quality of instruction, student-faculty relations, curricular variety, and student friendships. Although the continued existence of single-sex colleges in many ways may seem anachronistic, it is evident that they offer truly distinctive environments and that their potential to affect students and bring about change is greater than that of coeducational colleges.

Minority (Two Values). Institutions were categorized as minority if at least 50 percent of their enrollment was nonwhite and as nonminority if less than 50 percent of their enrollment was nonwhite. The variable of minority is related to organizational goals, activities, and normative order of institutions.

Assigning values to institutions in the 1980 sample was done by using institutional data compiled by the U.S. Office of Civil Rights, based upon a census conducted in 1978 (*The Chronicle of Higher Education,* Feb. 2, 1981). Data on the ethnic distribution of students in colleges and universities was not collected by any agency until the late 1960s, and therefore strictly comparable data cannot be obtained. However, a research project studying predominantly black institutions compiled an inventory in 1963 (McGrath, 1965) that was believed to include all colleges and universities existing then that enrolled a student body that was at least 50 percent black. In the absence of better data, this inventory was used to code the

1960 institutions in this study. It is believed that in the study states, there were no institutions that in 1960 enrolled a majority of nonwhite students who were not black.

Three types of institutions in the study sample predominantly enrolled minority students: traditionally black colleges located primarily in southern states; public and some private colleges with 50 percent or more of their enrollment being minority students but not belonging to the traditional black colleges' grouping (for example, Medgar Evers and Hostos colleges in New York City); and privately controlled colleges with a strong orientation to a particular ethnic constituency for whom the traditional academic structure of most colleges does not appear appropriate (for example, Universidad Boricua in New York City).

The traditional black colleges are believed to differ from predominantly white ones with regard to their ability to provide developmental and remedial instruction for students seriously underprepared for college-level academic work, their success at combining the liberal arts tradition and vocational education to complement rather than compete with each other, and their tendency to emphasize education's goals and purposes rather than its methods and techniques (Willie and Edmonds, 1978). Astin's (1977) longitudinal study of college freshmen revealed mixed results of the impact of predominantly black colleges upon their students compared to the impact of predominantly white institutions upon their black students. Attending a black college has positive effects upon the implementation of career plans in the fields of college teaching, nursing, medicine, and science. Students at black colleges are more satisfied with the social life but less satisfied with student-faculty relations than are black students at predominantly white colleges (Astin, 1977, p. 237). One important effect of black institutions is that the dropout rate for their students is substantially lower than that for black students at predominantly white institutions (Astin, 1975).

Community-based colleges established to serve a particular ethnic group are a fairly recent development in higher education. These institutions attempt to offer an alternative to minorities who feel alienated from even traditional institutions whose clientele are mostly minority group members. Rather than attempting to assimilate their students into the mainstream, these institutions provide an educational program closely identified with their students' cultural and language background. The students they attract are nontraditional, often older, working adults, able to attend only part-time, and many have been unsuccessful at publicly controlled community colleges (Smith and Bernstein, 1979). Students attending these colleges perceive them as being more concerned with individualized attention, having a learning-community environment, and espousing an ideology of cultural pluralism (Malcolm King Harlem College Extension, 1975, cited in Smith and Bernstein, 1979, p. 96). These colleges serve a very small percentage of the minority group students enrolled in colleges. However, the fact that these students are willing to pay tuition rather than attend low-cost public community colleges (Smith and Bernstein, 1979) indicates that the latter schools may not serve fully the needs of many minority students, perhaps because of their large size, impersonality, and lack of services to meet atypical student interests and needs. Minority institutions help students retain a strong identity with a culture and/or language that may be unfamiliar to a majority of students, faculty, and personnel in most nonminority colleges.

Defining Institutional Types

Many previous considerations of the concept of diversity tended to be unidimensional. Defining institutional type by the values of a single variable, the considerations often focused upon the distribution of values of that variable or the degree to which its distribution has changed over time. For example, the often-stated (but by no means proven) belief that diversity is primarily a function of the availability of private institutions has led to concerns that diversity may be decreasing as the proportion or number of private institutions decreases. Changes in other variables that often have been linked to a reduction in diversity are the sexual composition of the student body (smaller numbers of single-sex institutions), institutional size (loss of small-enrollment institutions), and program (smaller proportions of liberal arts colleges).

There are several major problems with unidimensional considerations of diversity. First, the considerations are usually based upon some ideological orientation that makes certain changes "good" and others "bad." For example, common understandings of diversity suggest that diminishing the number of private institutions decreases diversity but that decreasing the number of public institutions does not. Similarly, reducing the number of small institutions is somehow seen as more destructive of diversity than reducing the number of large ones, and changing teacher's colleges into multipurposed ones may be thought desirable while turning liberal arts colleges into comprehensive institutions is not—even though in both cases a distinctive institutional form may be lost. Another problem is that usually so few a number of values of the variables are used in such studies that potentially significant changes go unnoticed. Finally, unidimensional definitions ignore all aspects of diversity except the single one under consideration, and thus they may erroneously conclude from changes in that variable that diversity in general is decreasing.

When diversity is considered on two dimensions rather than one, many of the problems of ignoring important dimensions remain, but the method does provide better means of defining and measuring. For example, characterizing institutions solely according to size (small, medium, large) creates three possible institutional types; characterizing solely according to control (public, independent, religious, proprietary) creates four types. Combining these two variables into a two-dimensional array creates 3 X 4 institutional types defined by twelve unique combinations of size and control values. No one would claim that these twelve combinations exhaust all reasonable definitions of institutional type, but a two-dimensional definition does create a taxonomy with two major characteristics that suggest its superiority to a taxonomy based upon a single variable. First, a greater number of types are identified, so the taxonomy is therefore more sensitive to changes in the population. Second, because there is less tendency to identify one type as "better" than another, there is a focus upon the distribution (diversity) of types and changes in that distribution rather than upon whether they are moving in "good" or "bad" directions.

Thus moving from a one- to a two-dimensional analysis significantly refines the concept of institutional type. The concept can be extended still further by adding a third dimension. If, for example, the variable degree level with four values (two-year, four-year, master's or first professional, doctor's) is selected and combined with all combinations of values for size and control, 3 X 4 X 4, or forty-eight, different institutional types can be defined. All institutions in a population can be identified as belonging to one, and only one, of the forty-eight possible institutional types. For the purposes of studying diversity, it is not necessary to understand *why* small, public, two-year institutions are different from, say, large, church-related doctoral institutions, only that they represent different institutional forms that will react differently to the environment and that occupy different niches. In the same way, each of the forty-eight institutional types is different from the other on one, two, or all three variables, in some important way.

It is easy to agree that one institution is much different than another with which it does not share a single attribute (for example, a small, private, baccalaureate institution is a different type than a large, public, two-year one). At the same time, evidence has already been presented that large institutions have different effects than small ones, public ones different than private schools, and two-year institutions different than four-year schools. Institutions that share none of the values of the three variables not only are different from each other, but those that differ from each other on two of these variables, or only one, are also different. This is the rationale for considering each of the forty-eight types of institutions in this simple example as different.

This concept of defining types objectifies and simplifies the categorization of institutions and establishes a means of enumeration and analysis. At the same time, it begs certain important questions, among them degree of differentiation. Even if it can be argued that institutions of one type offer an educational environment different in some way from that at other types of institutions, there is a question about the comparative significance of these differences. Is a large, *public,* two-year institution more or less different from a large, *private,* two-year college than a *small,* public, two-year college is from a *large,* public, two-year college? Additionally, are differences *between* types greater or lesser than differences *within* types? That is, is it possible that small, public, two-year colleges are more different individually from each other than they are as a group from large, public, two-year colleges? This question becomes particularly important because some of the values of the variables are arbitrary and could be extended or compressed with reasonable grounds. As an example, combining all public institutions into one category of control ignores conceivably important differences among institutions controlled by federal, state, or local groups or, in some cases, combinations of these groups. The situation is even more dramatic in the case of religious control; the National Center for Education Statistics (1981b) identified seventy different religious sponsors of colleges or universities. There are even differences among sponsors of the same religion; Catholic institutions, for example, are controlled by individual orders and function without any centralized coordination from the church. Neither the issues of degree of differentiation nor between-type versus within-type differences can be resolved in this study. Recognizing that every institutional type is different in some way from every other, but having no data that definitively indicate the relative importance of these differences, this study treats all differences as being equally important. At the same time, to some extent it is possible to reduce the within- and between-type problem (but by no means eliminate it) by increasing the number of types so that between-type variance is increased and within-type variance decreased.

Conceptually, it is possible to define an institutional type in *N* rather than three dimensions. The number of unique institutional types is then equal to the product of all the values of all the variables, and each institution within the population can be identified as belonging to one, and only one, of the institutional types. By increasing sufficiently the number of variables and their values, it is possible to define a number of institutional types so large that not only are they more numerous than the total number of actual institutions, but in fact there are no two institutions of the same type. This would make the methodology unusable for the purposes of studying diversity. Therefore, when selecting the number of variables *N* that will be used to define types, care must be taken that the number is large enough to permit adequate differentiation between types but small enough to permit clustering of similar institutions within types.

The selection of the six variables already defined appears to meet these constraints. Together they create $3 \times 4 \times 2 \times 4 \times 4 \times 2$, or 768, potential institutional types.

Selecting the Sample

The population was sampled by selecting eight states and including all degree-granting institutions existing either in 1960, 1980, or in both years in those states. Selection of the states was based upon the assumption that certain state characteristics that might themselves influence diversity should be represented. These variables included size (the number of institutions in the state), geographical location, and state higher education coordinating structure. States were also selected so that a wide range of values of these variables were included.

Size. All fifty states were identified by size (number of institutions), with thirty or fewer colleges and universities in 1980 (National Center for Education Statistics, 1980b) considered small, between thirty-one and ninety institutions medium, and ninety-one or more institutions large. The final sample included four large and four medium states; small states were not included, because of the problems of considering diversity when there is only a handful of institutions and because almost all small states shared a similar state coordinating structure.

Geography. States were selected so that two each were included from the northeast, the south, the midwest, and the west.

Coordinating Structure. State higher education coordinating structure was identified as either consolidated governing board or coordinating board, as defined by the Education Commission of the States (1980, p. 6), with coordinating boards further divided into those with and without program-approval authority. Three states were selected from among those with consolidated governing boards, three with coordinating boards with program-approval authority, and two with coordinating boards without program-approval authority.

The Final Sample. The final sample included the eight states identified in Table 1. Although the states in the sample

Table 1. Sample of States Based on Size, Location, and State Governance Structure.

	Governing Structure and Size					
	Consolidated		*Coord. with Program Approval*		*Coord. without Program Approval*	
Geographical Location	*Medium*	*Large*	*Medium*	*Large*	*Medium*	*Large*
Northeast		Massachusetts		New York		
South	Florida		Virginia			
Midwest	Wisconsin					Michigan
West				Texas	Washington	

were not selected randomly, in many ways the institutions within them appear to reflect the population of higher education institutions in this country. Compared to all institutions in the country, those in this sample increased by number in about the same proportions between 1960 and 1980, had a comparable distribution by enrollment size in 1980 (1960 data not available), had similar distribution by public and nonpublic control in 1960 and 1980, offered the same degree levels in 1980 (1960 data not available), and had much the same distributions by sex of student body. Although the sample cannot be considered nationally representative because of the selection procedure, there is reason to believe that generalizations based upon it provide insights into higher education as a whole.

Within these eight states, all recognized colleges and universities were identified for 1960 using accepted standard references (U.S. Department of Health, Education and Welfare, 1960; *American Junior Colleges,* 1960; *American Universities and Colleges,* 1960); for 1980, the selection was based upon the schools' inclusion in the National Center for Education Statistics' *Education Directory* (1980c), supplemented as necessary by other reference sources (*Barron's Profiles of American Colleges,* 1980; *The College Handbook 1979–80,* 1979; *The College Blue Book,* 1979; National Center for Education Statistics, 1979, 1981). The 1960 data file therefore includes data collected anywhere between 1959 and 1961, and the 1980 data file is based upon data collected between 1978 and 1980.

The 1960 and 1980 files are not strictly comparable since the criteria by which institutions were included in the federal institutional census were different in both years. Earlier federal directories included institutions "offering at least a 2-year program of college-level studies" (U.S. Department of Health, Education and Welfare, 1967, p. 1). By 1980, the definition for inclusion was "offering at least a one-year program of college-level studies leading towards a degree" (National Center for Education Statistics, 1981b, p. vii). This change meant that included in the 1980 file were institutions (most commonly yeshivas under Jewish auspices) that existed but were not listed in the 1960 file. Such changes in definition artificially inflate the reported "growth" of the nonpublic sector during the twenty-year period and also confound attempts to measure *changes* in diversity. It was therefore decided to eliminate from both files all institutions listed in 1960 or 1980 as nondegree granting or offering less than two years of instruction. The price of achieving comparability in the files was therefore a small loss in the recorded levels of diversity in both years.

Table 2 enumerates these institutions. There were 614 institutions in the eight states in 1960, of which 493 (80.3 percent) still existed in 1980 but 121 did not. (Those 121

Table 2. Comparison of Institutions, 1960–1980.

	Existed in 1980	*Didn't Exist in in 1980*	*Total*
Existed in 1960	493	121	614
Didn't exist in 1960	392		
Total	885		

institutions no longer in existence failed, or they merged with another institution, thereby losing their identity.) By 1980, there were 885 total institutions, 392 (44.3 percent) of which were new. What appears to be the 44.1 percent growth of the system from 614 to 885 in twenty years is actually the result of a complex dynamic of institutional birth, death, and transformation. The loss of 121 institutions during the twenty-year period from the original base of 614 equates to a mortality rate of 98.5 per 10,000 per year, slightly higher than the comparable figures reported in Chapter One. This of course does not include institutions that failed before 1980 but were not in the sample because they were founded after 1960.

The values of each of the six variables were then determined for each institution in the sample as of 1960 and as of 1980. For the most part, the coding, although occasionally frustrating, was straightforward. Changes of definitions over time made it necessary in some cases to deviate from original sources. When, for example, the federal reporting system in 1960 treated identifiable campuses as a single institution but in 1980 treated them as separate institutions because of changes in definitions or the listing of branch campuses, the 1960 data were recoded to reflect their separate identities.

The one major deviation from federal definitions in 1980 was the identification of source of control. During the twenty-year period, a number of institutions changed control from religious to independent. For some schools, this was a major strategic change, in which religious values, programs, structures, and purposes were replaced by secular ones. For other institutions, however, there were other reasons for change in legal source of control, among the most prominent an institution's desire to be eligible to receive public support—an issue of particular moment in New York State when the so-called Bundy Law of 1969 provided public support to independent institutions based upon the number and types of degrees awarded. Institutions under the control or direction of a religious denomination or engaged in the teaching of a denominational doctrine or tenet were not eligible. In 1969, only 57 of the 100 potentially eligible institutions received aid. By 1978-79, 90 of the 119 potentially eligible institutions were aided (State Education Department, 1979). Many of those institutions changed their legal status from religious to independent control during that period.

It is not always easy to assess the consequences of such a legal change. As an example, Yeshiva University in New York was listed as under religious control in 1960 but legally considered independent in 1980. In 1980, however, the president of the institution was a rabbi; the school drew its undergraduate students mainly from orthodox Jewish homes; there were no non-Jewish undergraduates in the institution; and in addition to studying a secular major, all students were required to pursue four years of Judaic studies, including the study of Hebrew (Maeroff, 1981). Fordham University has a more eclectic student body and a less obvious religious-program emphasis. It too changed from religious to independent control, yet its president is a priest, and it is generally referred to as a Catholic university run by Jesuits (Briggs, 1981).

Evidence shows that religiously controlled institutions that become independent also change in other ways (Anderson, 1977). Yet clearly, in some cases the change is a distinction without a great difference. To automatically consider an institution as not religiously controlled because of its new legal status as an independent, nonprofit corporation appears to ignore the realities of institutional life. It therefore was decided to look individually at each institution that was coded as religiously controlled in 1960 but independent in 1980. If the senior executive officer of the institution and/or a majority of other officers were identified as religious (National Center for Education Statistics, 1980c), the institution was recoded to identify it as religious in 1980 rather than independent.

Classifying each institution according to the six variables considered in the study allows two major analyses. Chapter Five indicates the changes in the population that occurred during this twenty-year period, with particular attention to the differences caused by changes in existing institutions, the loss of institutions by demise or merger, and the creation of new institutions. In Chapter Six, these same variables are combined, to compare the distribution of institutional types during the two time periods and examine changes in institutional diversity.

5

Two Decades of Change in College Characteristics

The period between 1960 and 1980 was one of enormous growth in American higher education. The burgeoning of enrollments, campuses, and programs tends to obscure the fact that even in the midst of unprecedented plenty, not all institutions prospered. Many institutions were created, yet a smaller but significant number failed, and still others changed one or more of their basic characteristics in response to a changing environment. This chapter describes and analyzes the nature of these changes for the six variables. A common format is followed for each variable. First, the distribution of institutions on each variable is described and contrasted for the two study years; then an analysis is made of the transitional processes that account for the observed changes.

Control

In 1960, the population of higher education institutions was primarily nonpublic. The most obvious change in the distribution of institutions by control during the twenty-year study period, as shown in Table 3, was both the numerical and proportional increase in the population of public colleges and universities. The growth from 234 to 410 institutions during this period was a startling 75 percent. Expansion of the public sector has been a widely noted phenomenon; less commented upon are the significant increases in both the number and proportion of independent institutions. Their increase from 158 to 250 (58 percent) was somewhat offset by the small decrease in the number of religiously controlled institutions, whose representation was reduced from over a third of all institutions in 1960 to about one fifth in 1980. Religious control was the only one of the four categories of institution whose population diminished absolutely during the twenty-year period.

In the public and independent sectors, changes in numbers of institutions were accomplished primarily through the development of new colleges and universities. In all, 212 new public institutions were established (excluding those that were created after 1960 but failed prior to 1980)—a number almost equal to the total number of public institutions existing in 1960. During the same period, 105 new independent institutions were founded. At the same time, in both the public and independent sectors, institutions failed by either merging with another institution and losing their identity or disappearing altogether. The failure of independent institutions has been noted with alarm, but the failure of public institutions has occurred with little or no notice. The thirty-eight public institutions that failed between 1960 and 1980 represented 16 percent of all public institutions in the base year; the failure rate of independent institutions was only slightly higher at 18 percent! These comparisons ignore the failure rate of religiously controlled institutions, which was 23 percent. If religious and independent institutions are combined (as they often are when speaking generically of "private" higher education), the failure rate was 21 percent.

These data can be transformed into institutional mortality rates to permit comparisons among sectors and between historical periods. The mortality rate for the entire sample of institutions existing in 1960 was 98.5 per 10,000 per year, a level not unreasonably higher than the historical data reported in

Table 3. Changes in Institutional Control, 1960–1980.

			Transition (3)							
	1960 (2)		New		Failed		Change		1980 (4)	
Control (1)	*No.*	*%*	*No.*	*%*	*No.*	*%*	*To*	*From*	*No.*	*%*
Public	234	38.1	212	54.1	38	31.4	+2	. . .	410	46.3
Independent	158	25.7	105	26.8	29	24.0	+20	–4	250	28.2
Religious	211	34.4	44	11.2	49	40.5	+2	–16	192	21.7
Proprietary	11	1.8	31	7.9	5	4.1	. . .	–4	33	3.7
Total	614	100.0	392	100.0	121	100.0	+24	–24	885	99.9

Note: Tables 3 through 8 in this chapter have four major columns. Column 1 lists the values of the variable being analyzed. Here, the variable control has four possible values. Column 2 is the distribution of all institutions existing in the eight sample states in 1960. Under column 3, transition, are new institutions, those founded subsequent to 1960 and still in existence in 1980; failed institutions, those existing in 1960 but that either disappeared or lost their identity through merger by 1980; and change, a tally of the number of institutions existing in both 1960 and 1980 but that changed their control status during that period. Column 4 is the distribution of all institutions in the sample states as of 1980.

Using the control value of "public" as an example, the table can be read across rows as follows. In 1960, there were 234 public colleges and universities in the sample states, representing 38.1 percent of all institutions. During the transition period between 1960 and 1980, 212 new public institutions were created (equivalent to 54.1 percent of all new institutions), 38 public institutions failed (31.4 percent of all failures), two nonpublic institutions came under public control, and no public institution moved away from its public status. As a consequence of these changes, there were 410 public institutions in 1980, representing 46.3 percent of all institutions in the sample.

The 1980 number was computed simply. There were 234 institutions in 1960. Add to that 212 new institutions, subtract 38 failed institutions, add 2 institutions that changed to public status, and subtract 0 institutions leaving public status. The result is 410, the number of public institutions existing in 1980.

Chapter One. The mortality rate for public institutions during the twenty-year study period was 81.2 per 10,000, and for private institutions (independent and religious combined), 105.7 per 10,000. By comparison, Zammuto's (1983a) mortality rates presented in Chapter One were prepared based on data from 1971 and 1981, using the total national population of 2,881 institutions completing federal reporting forms. His analysis indicated a total mortality rate of 96.8 per 10,000 (almost identical to the 98.5 per 10,000 found in this study). Zammuto calculated the private institution mortality rate as 118.6 per 10,000 (slightly higher than the 105.7 in the eight-state sample) and the public institution mortality rate as 65.7 per 10,000, which is moderately less than the 81.2 per 10,000 found in this study. Differences in the public sector mortality rates probably were caused by a sample bias introduced by the inclusion in this study of Wisconsin, a state with a disproportionate number of public institution closings. Even accepting the lower Zammuto data as more accurately representing national trends, it is evident that while public institutions may have had somewhat greater protection against failure than private ones, they have been much more vulnerable to the demands of their environments than has been generally supposed in the past.

The most volatile sector during the past twenty years has been proprietary institutions. Three times the number of new institutions were created during the study period as existed in 1960, but almost half of those that existed twenty years ago have failed. During this period, the proprietary institutions were increasingly legitimized by recognition of regional accrediting associations, degree-granting authority awarded by state agencies, and greater attention in the other sectors to the highly specialized vocational programming that once was the singular focus of the for-profit sector. For these reasons and because the number of institutions is still so small, the development of proprietary institutions over the past two decades probably gives a less reliable basis for estimating future trends than is true of the other sectors.

In Table 3 (and Tables 4 to 8), the change column indicates the number of institutions in each category that existed in both study years but that changed status during the twenty-year period. For example, two existing institutions changed their control to public between 1960 and 1980, an exceptionally small number, given recent concerns about incorporation of private institutions into public systems. The greatest amount of change occurred between the independent and religious sectors, with a clear tendency for religious institutions to move into independent status. This tendency would have been more pronounced had institutions that formally changed their legal status but appear to have retained their religious identity (such as Yeshiva University) been listed under their new status.

In all, only twenty-four institutions changed their control status during the period. No public institution changed to another category, and no institution of any kind changed to proprietary status. Other than these exceptions, all other possible changes took place. The extent of change, however, was less than for any other variable considered in this study; the probability that, once created, an institution is able to change its control is apparently extremely small.

Degree Level

In both 1960 and 1980, the most prevalent institutional form in terms of highest degree offered was the two-year college (see Table 4). The number of institutions increased in each of the four categories, but the increase of 217 two-year institutions during the two-decade period was also greater than in any other category. It was not the greatest proportional increase, however; that change occurred in doctoral-granting institutions, which increased in total number from 68 in 1960 to 127 in 1980, a change of 187 percent. Both four-year colleges and those offering master's degrees decreased in terms of their representation in the institutional population by 1980, even as they showed modest increases in total numbers.

The transitional changes between 1960 and 1980 are all consistent and form a clear pattern. The development of new institutions was inversely related to highest degree offered; a greater number and proportion of new institutions were two-

Table 4. Changes in Institutional Degree Level, 1960–1980.

Degree Level	1960		Transition: New		Transition: Failed		Transition: Change		1980	
	No.	*%*	*No.*	*%*	*No.*	*%*	*To*	*From*	*No.*	*%*
Two-year	217	35.3	226	57.7	75	62.0	+2	–29	341	38.5
Four-year	168	27.4	79	20.2	28	23.1	+34	–51	202	22.8
Master's	161	26.2	61	15.6	12	9.9	+54	–49	215	24.3
Doctor's	68	11.1	26	6.6	6	5.0	+41	–2	127	14.4
Total	614	100.0	392	100.1	121	100.0	+131	–131	885	100.0

year colleges than any other, and the fewest number and proportion of new institutions were those offering doctor's degrees. Failed institutions exhibited exactly the same relationship, with approximately 62 percent of them two-year colleges and only about 5 percent doctoral institutions. In other words, the more likely an institutional category was to have failed institutions, the more likely it was to have added new ones as well.

Because of the close correspondence between founding and failure rates by category, it would be expected that the growth in the number of graduate-level institutions would not occur exclusively through the development of new institutions. In fact, a large number of the new master's institutions, and the majority of the new doctoral institutions, were composed of colleges and universities that had changed their degree level between 1960 and 1980. With relatively few exceptions, the changes were all toward higher degree levels. For example, twenty-nine two-year colleges increased their degree level during this period, while only two institutions reduced it to offer only two-year degrees. At the other end of the distribution, forty-one institutions that had not done so in 1960 began offering a doctor's degree by 1980, and only two institutions that previously had offered doctor's degrees stopped doing so.

To some extent, the differentiation between institutions offering four-year and master's degrees is somewhat problematic because in at least some cases the master's degree may be an institutional anomaly offered in relatively few programs or to a small number of persons. It is difficult therefore to fully understand from these data the extent to which the shifting to and from these categories represents real change or is an artifact of nomenclature. It is clear, however, that at least at the extremes, degree level appears fairly stable. That is, two-year institutions tend to remain two-year institutions, and doctoral institutions also are unlikely to change. In the middle ranges, greater change takes place, but except for the movement into doctoral work, its extent and significance are unclear.

Program Type

Institutional programs were identified as liberal arts, comprehensive, professional/technical, or teacher education. Although teacher education could have been incorporated into the professional/technical category, it was separated because of the long history of institutions specifically identified as fulfilling this function. Table 5 breaks down institutions by curriculum type for 1960–1980.

In both 1960 and 1980, the most common institutional curriculum was comprehensive and offered both liberal arts programs and professional or technical degrees. These institutions experienced the greatest growth increase during the period as well, from 263 to 507 during the twenty-year period. As of the last study year, they comprised fully 57.3 percent of the institutions in the sample. The number of professional/technical institutions increased during this period at about the same rate as the total population, so that their proportional representation was stable over the study period.

The most significant changes were in institutions with liberal arts curriculums and those identified as primarily teacher preparatory. That the total representation of liberal arts colleges declined from 26.9 to 19.0 percent of the sample apparently supports recently stated concerns about the vulnerability of these institutions. However, the actual number of liberal arts colleges itself did not decrease during the period; in fact, there were slightly more such institutions in 1980 than in 1960. Institutions primarily concerned with teacher preparation, on the other hand, underwent a completely different kind of change. Small in number to begin with, and representing only 8.0 percent of the sample in 1960, they had completely disappeared by 1980. Of the six variables with eighteen different values included in this study, this is the only example in which a value represented in one time period did not appear in the other.

The transitions of institutions between curriculum area was particularly interesting. Conventional wisdom to the contrary, a reasonable number of new liberal arts colleges were founded during the period, although they represented only 13.0 percent of all new institutions. On the other hand, liberal arts colleges were no more likely to have failed during the period than were institutions of any other curriculum type; they comprised 26.9 percent of all institutions in 1960 and 25.6 percent of all institutional failures by 1980. And although fifty-eight

Table 5. Changes in Institutional Program, 1960–1980.

Curriculum Type	*1960*		*Transition*						*1980*	
			New		*Failed*		*Change*			
	No.	*%*	*No.*	*%*	*No.*	*%*	*To*	*From*	*No.*	*%*
Liberal arts	165	26.9	51	13.0	31	25.6	+41	–58	168	19.0
Comprehensive	263	42.8	215	54.8	37	30.6	+112	–46	507	57.3
Professional	137	22.3	126	32.1	26	21.5	+11	–38	210	23.7
Teacher prep.	49	8.0	. . .	. . .	27	22.3	. . .	–22	. . .	. . .
Total	614	100.0	392	99.9	121	100.0	+164	–164	885	100.0

institutions that had been liberal arts colleges moved into other categories during the twenty-year period, forty-one institutions that had offered other programs became liberal arts colleges. The oft-foretold demise of the liberal arts college appears, on the basis of these data, like the notice of Mark Twain's death: to have been greatly exaggerated. Although their proportional representation in the population of institutions did decline during the study period, they ended the twenty years with slightly greater numbers than they began. Their decreased representation was not caused by excessive failures or curriculum changes; it was caused by a rate of founding new institutions that was somewhat lower than that for institutions with other program emphases.

The growth of professional institutions generally paralleled that of all institutions in the population during the study period. They were somewhat more likely to have been founded as new institutions, somewhat more likely to have lost rather than gained due to institutions changing programs, and about as likely to fail as schools in other categories. They ended the twenty-year period with a proportional representation in the population about equal to what it was when they began.

The most successful of all the groups were those institutions with comprehensive programs. They began with the greatest number and proportion of institutions, experienced the greatest number and proportion of newly founded institutions, had the greatest number of existing institutions change their programs into that category, and ended the study period by almost doubling their total number and representing almost three of every five campuses in the sample. Although 37 of the original 263 comprehensive institutions (14.1 percent) also failed during the period, the failure rate was somewhat lower than that of liberal arts colleges (18.8 percent) or professional institutions (19.0 percent). Comprehensive programs therefore appeared to offer a modest competitive advantage during the period under study.

Although three of the program groups increased in number, proportional representation, or both during the study period, teacher preparatory institutions became extinct. Starting with the smallest number of institutions in 1960, by 1980, all either had failed or undergone a program transition, usually to become a comprehensive institution. No new institutions in this category were founded during the period.

Enrollment Size

Institutional size as measured by headcount enrollment is the only continuous variable considered in this study. The three size categories in Table 6 are therefore somewhat arbitrary. The categories were selected according to the reasons discussed in Chapter Four, but note that had different values been used for the three groupings, or a different number of groupings established altogether, the results, although similar, might have been different.

Small institutions of 1,000 enrollment or less constituted almost two thirds of the population in 1960 and just one third in 1980. The total number of small institutions decreased during the period from 384 to 303. The number of medium-sized institutions with enrollments between 1,000 and 2,500 increased parallel to the growth of the system as a whole, so that their representation as a proportion of the total population did not change appreciably between 1960 and 1980. By far both the greatest numerical and percentage increases were experienced by larger institutions, whose enrollments were over 2,500 students. Between the two study years, their numbers increased over four times and their representation in the population over three times; two of every five institutions in 1980 were identified as large.

The transitional processes during the twenty-year period were unidirectional and closely related to size. The increased number and proportion of large campuses were due partly to the fact that new campuses were more likely to be larger than those existing in 1960. Of even greater significance was the growth process of institutions between the two study years: Small institutions tended to get bigger, and very few large institutions tended to become small. The grouping of institutions into categories probably masks shifts at some institutions in

Table 6. Changes in Enrollment Size, 1960–1980.

Enrollment	1960		Transition						1980	
			New		Failed		Change			
	No.	%	No.	%	No.	%	To	From	No.	%
1–1,000	384	62.5	160	40.8	111	92.4	+2	−132	303	34.2
1,001–2,500	146	23.8	98	25.0	10	7.6	+86	−96	224	25.3
2,501 and up	84	13.7	134	34.2	. . .	. . .	+145	−5	358	40.5
Total	614	100.0	392	100.0	121	100.0	+233	−233	885	100.0

which enrollment was reduced; however, the probability that an institution that began 1960 with over 2,500 students would fall below that level was extremely small.

An additional significant factor in the change of size distribution was the failure rate of institutions. Of the 384 small institutions in 1960, 111 had failed by 1980—a mortality rate of 28.9 percent, or 289 per 10,000. In contrast, the mortality rate of medium-sized institutions was 34.2 per 10,000, and no institution of over 2,500 students failed.

Small institutional enrollment was clearly a major factor related to failure. At the same time, the increased vulnerability of size does not appear to have deterred the founding of new small colleges. Between 1960 and 1980, 160 new institutions were founded that still existed in the last study year and had enrollments of under 1,000 students. Since this is a high-mortality rate category, it would be expected that an additional number of such institutions were probably founded subsequent to 1960 and not included in these data because they had failed before 1980.

Sex of Student Body

The population was dominated by coeducational institutions in both study years, but both the number and proportion of single-sex institutions plummeted between 1960 and 1980, as shown in Table 7. There were 183 institutions enrolling men only or women only in 1960, representing almost 30 percent of the institutional population. By 1980, only fifty-five such institutions remained in the population. Because of the increase in the size of the total population, the decline in proportional representation of single-sex institutions was even more dramatic: By 1980 they represented only 6.2 percent of all institutions.

The change was affected by the extremely small rate of founding new single-sex institutions (only sixteen total) and the somewhat higher mortality rate (131.1 per 10,000 compared to 84.7 per 10,000 for coeducational institutions). The greatest single factor, however, was the movement of institutions that were single-sex in 1960 to coeducational status in 1980. In all,

Table 7. Changes in Sex of Student Body, 1960–1980.

Sex	1960		Transition						1980	
			New		*Failed*		*Change*			
	No.	*%*	*No.*	*%*	*No.*	*%*	*To*	*From*	*No.*	*%*
Coeducational	431	70.2	376	95.9	73	60.3	+97	−1	830	93.8
Male only	82	13.4	8	2.0	20	16.5	+1	−50	21	2.4
Female only	101	16.4	8	2.0	28	23.1	0	−47	34	3.8
Total	614	100.0	392	99.9	121	99.9	+98	−98	885	100.0

ninety-seven institutions made such a change, and only one that had been coeducational adopted a single-sex policy.

Minority Enrollment

Although institutions whose enrollments included at least 50 percent minority students were a small part of higher education in both study years, their numbers and proportional representation had increased significantly by 1980. Table 8 shows the total number of minority institutions in the sample increasing 169 percent, from twenty-six in 1960 to seventy twenty years later. Minority institutions were more likely to fail than were nonminority, but they were also more likely to be founded; 8.7 percent of all new institutions were minority, although they represented only 4.2 percent of all institutions in 1960.

Surprisingly, a good portion of the growth in minority institutions occurred because of changes in existing institutions. Twenty nonminority institutions in 1960 became minority by 1980, and in only one institution was the process reversed.

Summary

The changes in the characteristics of the population of institutions between 1960 and 1980 are not remarkable to anyone familiar with trends in American higher education over the past twenty years, although some of the dynamics leading to these changes are surprising. In general, institutions at the end of the study period compared to the beginning tended more often to be public and less often to be controlled by religious groups, to have moved toward offering higher-degree levels, to have comprehensive programs, to have increased in size, and to be coeducational. This simple analysis, primarily based upon comparing frequency distributions for the two study years, masks the often turbulent dynamics of the system. Institutions do not merely exist in different states during two different years; they are also created, and they fail and/or change in numerous ways. The summary data record the temporary out-

Table 8. Changes in Minority Status, 1960–1980.

	1960		Transition: New		Transition: Failed		Transition: Change		1980	
Status	*No.*	*%*	*No.*	*%*	*No.*	*%*	*To*	*From*	*No.*	*%*
Minority	26	4.2	34	8.7	9	7.4	+20	−1	70	7.9
Nonminority	588	95.8	358	91.3	112	92.6	+1	−20	815	92.1
Total	614	100.0	392	100.0	121	100.0	+21	−21	885	100.0

comes of the effects of these changes at specific time periods. When the intervening activities are also considered, it becomes clear that statements of general trends can be misleading. Even while some institutions can be changing one of their characteristics, such as curriculum, in a direction that moves them toward the population norm, others are moving from that position toward some other. An examination of the intervening dynamics leads to some findings of unusual interest, including:

The public sector increased during the period, but not at the expense of the private sector, which also grew—albeit at a somewhat slower rate.

Newly created colleges were predominantly two-year institutions, but despite the development of a large number of new institutions during the period, the proportional representation of two-year colleges increased only slightly. This seeming contradiction was created by a disproportionately high failure rate among two-year institutions and a slight tendency for some of them to expand their programs to higher-degree levels.

The number of liberal arts institutions increased slightly during the period, although their proportional representation decreased because relatively few new ones were founded.

More institutions were large than was true in the past, but fully a third of the population still enrolled under 1,000 students and newly created institutions still tended to be small rather than large. Despite their higher mortality rate, small institutions still represent a major, although declining, grouping of institutions in the population.

The transition from moderate representation of single-sex institutions to miniscule representation occurred because of the changed policies of existing institutions.

Changes in these various categories were therefore caused by different factors. In some cases, they occurred because of the distribution of new institutions, in others because of the changes made by existing institutions, and in still others by the institutions' failure to survive. Because of this study's emphasis upon the processes of selection, the identification of characteristics associated with institutional failure is of particular interest. Factors that were associated with a higher-than-average probability of institutional mortality were two-year degree level, teacher-preparatory curriculum, religious control, small enrollment, and single-sex enrollment. Factors commonly thought to be related to failure either were not (for example, liberal arts curriculum) or were not as important as previously supposed (for example, independent control). And characteristics that initially appear to provide unusual competitive advantage that might lead to significantly decreased rates of institutional failure, such as public control or professional/technical program, upon analysis do not seem to provide the level of protection previously assumed. It should be noted, however, that these findings are based upon single-variable analyses, which can be misleading. The apparent vulnerability of two-year colleges, for example, becomes clearer when these institutions are further divided by source of control and the mortality of *private* junior colleges is highlighted.

Of all the variables examined, the one that appears most closely related to institutional survival is enrollment size. Small institutions, particularly those of 500 enrollment and under, lead a precarious existence within the population. In this study, of the 277 institutions with under 500 enrollment in 1960, 37.4 percent failed and 41.7 percent increased in size by 1980. Only 20.9 percent survived the entire twenty years without changing enrollment category. The message for such small institutions appears to be "grow or die."

Examining the data presented in this chapter illuminates the problems of attempting to evaluate levels and changes in diversity through single-variable analyses of population characteristics. Does the existence of a greater number of institutions signify greater diversity? From the perspective of diversity, is a decline in religious control offset by the development of the relatively new proprietary sector? Does a greater number of comprehensive institutions suggest that diversity is increasing or decreasing? There is no way to answer these questions based upon these kinds of data.

Measuring diversity and its changes requires a different kind of analytic approach. The following chapter describes the development of the approach and the measurement of changes in diversity in the population.

6 Changes in Types of Institutions Since 1960

Following the discussion in Chapter Four, institutional types (the organizational analogue to biological species) were defined in terms of possible combinations of six organizational variables. Using these variables, it is possible to develop an exhaustive and inclusive classification of institutional types that can be structured into a matrix.

If institutional types are defined by the values of only two variables, such a matrix is the graph of these variables along two axes. Every institution in the population can be assigned to one, and only one, of the cells created by the graph. Similarly, three variables can be combined to form a three-dimensional space consisting of all possible combinations of the variables.

Although more difficult to "see," it is possible to conceptualize an *N*-dimensional hyperspace, in which each cell is defined by the coordinates of the axes of *N* variables. This matrix includes all possible combinations of the *N* variables and thus by definition includes all institutional types that potentially could exist in a population.

In this study, the matrix of institutional types is defined by six variables: control, program, degree level, size, sex, and minority. The number of cells in the matrix is determined by cross multiplying the number of values of each variable, in this case, 4 X 4 X 4 X 3 X 2 X 2, respectively, for a total of 768 potential types. It is possible to take the entire population, or any sample, and assign each institution to one of these 768 cells based upon the values of these six variables. The result of this categorization is called the diversity matrix.

A number of calculations can be performed after institutions have been placed into their appropriate cells in the diversity matrix. For example, the number of cells *actually* occupied can be counted (determining the number of different institutional types in the sample), the number of actual types can be compared to the number of potential types, and the number of institutions in each cell can be compared to determine which types have a larger or smaller representation. Such calculations can be used to examine the issue of diversity. Consider a situation in which all institutions in a sample share exactly the same values of the six variables in this study and thus are all assigned to only one of the 768 cells in the matrix. This is a situation of minimum diversity, since the smallest number of cells is occupied, and the maximum number of institutions is in a single cell. On the other hand, if each institution in a sample has a different combination of values of the six variables and thus is assigned to a different cell of the diversity matrix, this is a maximum diversity, since the greatest number of cells is occupied, and each cell contains the smallest possible number of institutions.

The diversity matrix is therefore a means of examining the distribution of institutional types within a population or sample. In this study, diversity is defined as a function of the concentration and dispersal of institutions within the diversity matrix; diversity increases as concentration decreases and dispersion increases. Note that although for the purposes of this study 768 distinct potential institutional types are assumed, to a great extent the number of cells in the diversity matrix is an artifact of the number of variables and the values of these variables, as selected by the researcher. Eliminating degree level as a variable, for example, reduces the number of cells to 192; changing the values of the variable "size" from three to six increases the cells to 1,536. As discussed later, however, the measurement of diversity itself may not be particularly sensitive to the number of cells in the matrix.

Several major questions are considered in this chapter. How were institutions in the sample of eight states distributed in the diversity matrix in 1960 and 1980? How can the distribution of institutions within the matrix be quantified and measured to permit analysis and comparison between time periods and among the states in the sample? What institutional types have undergone the greatest changes in their representation in the sample during the twenty-year study period? How can a quantified index of diversity be used in policy research?

Distribution of Institutional Types

Each institution in the population in 1960 was assigned to one cell of the diversity matrix, based upon the values of six variables. Table 9 shows the number of types of institutions and the number of institutions of each existing type. The listing is by size, so the cells with the greatest population (that is, the types with the greatest numbers of institutions) are listed first.

In 1960, there were 614 different institutions in the eight-state sample. If those institutions were completely diverse, each would occupy a different cell in the diversity matrix, and there would be 614 institutional types. If the sample were completely homogeneous, all 614 would be in the same cell, and only one institutional type would be represented. Table 9 indicates that the actual situation in 1960 was somewhere between these two extremes: The 614 institutions were placed in 141 different cells in the diversity matrix and thus represented 141 distinct institutional types.

The distribution of both types and institutions can be determined by reading across the table. In the first row, for example, the data show one institutional type that included within it fifty-three institutions. This was the single type with the largest

Table 9. Distribution of Institutional Types and Number of Institutions of Each Type, 1960.

Number of Types	*Number of Institutions in Type*	*Cumulative Number of Types*		*Cumulative Number of Institutions*	
		No.	*%*	*No.*	*%*
1	53	1	0.7	53	8.6
1	35	2	1.4	88	14.3
1	24	3	2.1	112	18.2
1	22	4	2.8	134	21.8
1	18	5	3.5	152	24.8
1	16	6	4.3	168	27.4
2	15	8	5.7	198	32.2
1	13	9	6.1	211	34.4
1	12	10	7.1	223	36.3
1	11	11	7.8	234	38.1
1	10	12	8.5	244	39.7
3	9	15	10.6	271	44.1
4	8	19	13.5	303	49.3
7	7	26	18.4	352	57.3
4	6	30	21.3	376	61.2
11	5	41	29.1	431	70.2
11	4	52	36.9	475	77.4
13	3	65	46.1	514	83.7
24	2	89	63.1	562	91.5
52	1	141	100.0	614	100.0
141		141	100.0	614	100.0

concentration of institutions in the sample; although that one type was only 0.7 percent of the observed types, it had within it 8.6 percent of the total institutions. Reading down the columns indicates the declining number of institutions within types. The next largest type had thirty-five institutions, and in total, twelve types were represented by ten or more institutions each. Although there were some large clusters of institutions by type, there was also a substantial number of institutions (fifty-two) that were singlets, or the only representative of their type.

Table 10 is a similar analysis for 1980. The total number of institutions represented in 1980 was 885, a growth of 44.1 percent from 1960, but the total number of institutional types declined from 141 in 1960 to 138 in 1980. At the same time,

Table 10. Distribution of Institutional Types and Number of Institutions of Each Type, 1980.

Number of Types	*Number of Institutions in Type*	*Cumulative Number of Types*		*Cumulative Number of Institutions*	
		No.	*%*	*No.*	*%*
1	123	1	0.7	123	13.9
1	58	2	1.4	181	20.5
1	47	3	2.2	228	25.8
1	37	4	2.9	265	29.9
1	27	5	3.6	292	33.0
1	25	6	4.3	317	35.8
1	20	7	5.1	337	38.1
3	19	10	7.2	394	44.5
1	18	11	8.0	412	46.6
1	17	12	8.7	429	48.5
2	15	14	10.1	459	51.9
1	14	15	10.9	473	53.4
2	13	17	12.3	499	56.4
4	12	21	15.2	547	61.8
1	11	22	15.9	558	63.1
1	10	23	16.7	568	64.2
1	9	24	17.4	577	65.2
4	8	28	20.3	609	68.8
6	7	34	24.6	651	73.6
6	6	40	29.0	687	77.6
6	5	46	33.3	717	81.0
11	4	57	41.3	761	86.0
11	3	68	49.3	794	89.7
21	2	89	64.5	836	94.5
49	1	138	100.0	885	100.0
138	885	138	100.0	885	100.0

the size of the type with the greatest number of institutions substantially increased from 8.6 percent in 1960 to 13.9 percent in 1980. At the other end of the spectrum, the number and proportion of singlets were less in 1980 than in 1960.

A decline in the number of institutional types, a decline in the number and proportion of singlets, and an increase in the proportion of institutions located in the largest institutional type all suggest a decline in diversity between 1960 and 1980. However, the data do not consider such factors as the growth in the number of institutions in the sample during the two periods, and thus they have significant limitations for the purpose of analysis. Are there simple ways of measuring the concentration and dispersion of institutions within types so that reliable comparisons can be made between the two years? Biologists concerned with measuring and comparing diversity in different ecological communities, or changes in diversity in the same community over time, are faced with the same question. They have developed several ways of making these comparisons, the simplest merely enumerating the number of species found in a community. More sophisticated measures relate the number of species in a sample to the number of individuals in each species. Several procedures and formulas for analyzing these relationships have been developed, each yielding comparable results, so none appears necessarily preferable to another (Krebs, 1972). Statistical analyses of organizational diversity can be based up on the same methodologies population ecologists have developed.

Measuring Diversity, 1960-1980: Simple Indices

The data in Tables 9 and 10 suggest several possible ways diversity can be measured and an index of diversity developed. Four possibilities—indices A, B, C, and D, respectively—are now described.

Index A. Diversity increases as institutions are spread over a larger number of types. To calculate index A, divide the number of institutions in the sample by the number of types they represent. Where the number of institutions is the same as the number of types, index A is 1.00, reflecting maximum diversity. The upper limit of the index is equal to the total number of institutions in the sample, assuming that in a situation of least diversity they are all in the same cell of the diversity matrix. Index A is thus inversely related to diversity: The higher the index, the less the diversity.

Index B. Diversity increases as large-scale clustering within the most densely populated cell of the matrix decreases. To calculate index B, divide the number of institutions in the most densely populated cell of the matrix by the total number of institutions in the sample (and multiply by 100 for ease of calculation). Index B is inversely related to diversity: The greater the clustering of institutions in the densest cell in the matrix, the less the level of diversity.

Index C. Diversity increases as the concentration of institutions within types decreases. Taking an arbitrary proportion of institutional types in the sample (say, 10 percent), diversity is then inversely related to the proportion of institutions that are located within the densest 10 percent of the cells in the matrix. In the least diverse situation, 99.9 percent of the institutions are in 10 percent of the cells; in the most diverse situation, 10 percent of the institutions are in 10 percent of the cells. To determine the index, merely calculate the proportion of institutions in the sample that are in the most highly populated 10 percent of the cells of the diversity matrix and multiply by 100 for ease of calculation.

Index D. Diversity increases as the proportion of institutions in a sample that belong to a cell in the matrix with no other institution (that is, that are unique representatives of an institutional type) increases. To calculate diversity index D, divide the number of institutional singlets by the total number of institutions in the population and multiply by 100 for ease of calculation. The index is directly related to diversity, with a value of 100 indicating maximum diversity (every institution in the sample is a singlet), and a value approaching zero indicating least diversity (no institution is a singlet).

Table 11 compares diversity levels in 1960 and 1980 as measured by these four diversity indices. The simple indices calculated indicate that on all four measures, diversity was greater in 1960 than in 1980. In general, it can be said that during the twenty-year study period, institutions became much more tightly clustered and much less widely dispersed throughout the diversity matrix. Whether looking at the number of such clusters, the size of the largest clusters, or the presence of types represented by single institutions, the results are the same: Diversity has in fact decreased. It is difficult to specify the magnitude of the decrease since the indices may not be equally sensitive to changes and there are no normative or comparative data that

Table 11. Calculation and Comparison of Four Simple Diversity Indices for 1960 and 1980.

Index	1960 Calculation	1960 Index	1980 Calculation	1980 Index
A: no. inst./no. types	614/141	4.4[a]	885/138	6.4
B. largest type/tot. inst. × 100	53/614 × 100	8.6[a]	123/885 × 100	13.9
C: inst. in 10% types/tot. inst.	263/614 × 100	42.8[a]	457/885 × 100	51.6
D: singlets/tot. inst. × 100	56/614 × 100	9.1[a]	49/885 × 100	5.5

[a]Indicates index reflecting higher diversity for each of the two study years.

can be used to validate them. However, a recognized technique called Lorenz curve analysis, which, although more complex than these simple measures, may also be more stable and combine some of the data used for the simpler indices.

Measuring Diversity, 1960–1980: Lorenz Curve Analysis

Lorenz curve analysis is a process by which the cumulative frequency of members of a sample is compared to the cumulative frequency of some other attribute of the population (such as wealth), to detect and analyze inequality. The joint distributions of the two cumulative frequencies can be plotted on a graph, with one variable on the *x* axis and one on the *y* axis, so that the degree of inequality can be seen visually and the actual degree of inequality measured. Bruno (1976) described the process.

In Figure 2, the cumulative frequency (expressed in percentages) of institutional types is on the *y* axis and the cumulative frequency of the number of institutions on the *x* axis. If diversity is "perfect," at any point in the distribution the cumulative percentage of institutional types and the cumulative percentage of institutions in those types are the same (that is, 10

Figure 2. Lorenz Curves Comparing Areas of Inequality for 1960 and 1980.

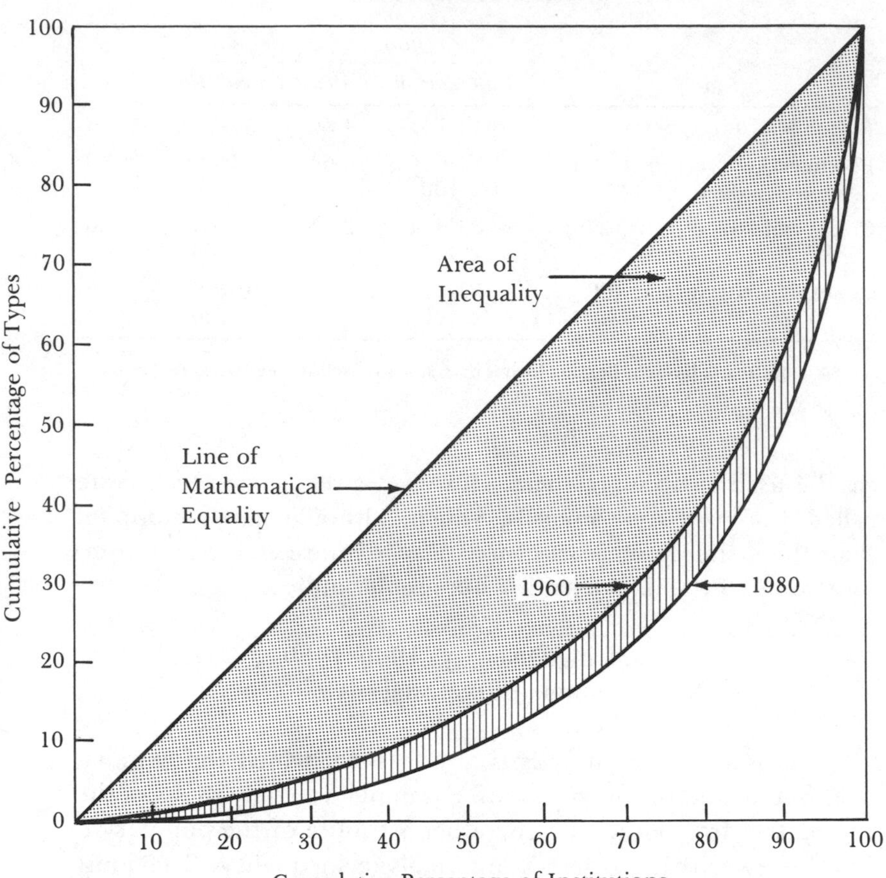

percent of the types include 10 percent of the institutions; 20 percent of the types include 20 percent of the institutions; and so on). In this context, the term perfect does not necessarily indicate that this distribution is desirable or normative but that it is the distribution that reflects maximum diversity according to the concepts of dispersion and lack of concentration within the diversity matrix. Given perfect diversity, the plotted values of the two variables form a line bisecting the graph at a 45° angle. That line is called the line of mathematical equality.

Plotting a relationship of other than perfect equality produces a line called the Lorenz curve, which has the same beginning and end point as the line of mathematical equality but is below it for all other values. The area between the Lorenz curve and the line of mathematical equality is called the area of inequality and can be used to measure the difference between the actual distribution and the perfect one.

Figure 2 shows Lorenz curves for institutions and types for both 1960 and 1980. The shaded portion indicates the area of inequality for 1960; the additional crosshatched area indicates the increased portion of the area of inequality for 1980. By inspection, the area of inequality is determined as larger for 1980 than for 1960. According to the definitions presented in this study, this reflects lesser diversity in 1980 than in 1960.

The exact amount of inequality in a Lorenz curve can be measured by the Gini index, which is equal to twice the shaded area of the graph divided by the total area of the graph. The Gini index can range from 0 (when there is perfect equality, the Lorenz curve and the line of mathematical equality are identical and therefore there is no shaded area) to 1 (when there is perfect inequality and the entire area under the line of mathematical equality is shaded). The areas under the line of mathematical equality were determined geometrically, and the Gini indices were calculated as .5502 in 1960 and .6321 in 1980. Since the Gini index is a measure of inequality, the data indicate that there was greater inequality (decreased diversity) in 1980 than in 1960. During the twenty-year period, the higher education system moved further away from maximum diversity than it had been in 1960.

An additional measure derived from the Lorenz curve is the minimal majority—the point at which institutional types account for at least 50 percent of the total institutions. Examination of Figure 2 indicates that the minimal majority in 1960 was 13.9 percent (that is, about 14 percent of the institutional types contained 50 percent of the institutional population); by 1980 the minimal majority had been reduced to 9.3 percent, another clear indication of increased concentration of institutions and, consequently, of decreased diversity.

Measuring Diversity—Simple Systems and the Gini Index

The Gini index offers a number of advantages to those wishing to measure changes in institutional diversity. It is based upon a mathematical model, it has known ranges, the importance of differences in the index can be evaluated within the context of this known range, and it is relatively stable.* Its major disadvantage is that it is cumbersome and time-consuming to compute and draw. Although it is possible without drawing to determine the index with the calculus, many potential users of a diversity measure would still find it difficult to construct.

On the other hand, a previous section developed four other indices: A, B, C, and D. They have the advantage of being relatively easy to compute, but it is difficult to know exactly what their measurements mean. Of major importance, their validity is uncertain as well. If, however, any of these indices could be shown as measuring the same characteristics of the system as the Gini index, the method might be a useful shortcut for analysis. To determine the validity of these four simple indices, the Gini index for 1960 and 1980 was prepared for each

*The four diversity indices A, B, C, and D are all related in one way or another to the total number of institutional types. As previously indicated, the number of types is itself an artifact of the data since it can be increased or decreased by changing either the number of values for any variable or the number of variables themselves. To determine the stability of the Gini index, four versions were calculated. The version used in this study is based upon six variables, leading to a total of 768 cells in the diversity matrix and therefore to 768 possible types. Three other versions were also calculated. In one version, the variable minority was eliminated, thus reducing the number of cells in the diversity matrix to 384. In the second version, the variable size was eliminated, leading to a matrix of 256 cells. In the third version, a new variable was added, to make a total of seven variables. This new variable was "regional accreditation," a status enjoyed by 63.3 percent of the population in 1960 and 85.9 percent in 1980. Inclusion of this dichotomous variable expanded the diversity matrix to 1,536 cells. When Lorenz curves were prepared for these four sets of data (five variables yielding 384 cells, five variables yielding 256 cells, six variables yielding 768 cells, and seven variables yielding 1,536 cells), they proved virtually identical! The Lorenz curve, and the consequent Gini index, therefore appear relatively stable and indifferent to the actual number of variables employed. The range of indifference is not known.

of the eight states in the sample. The index then correlated to the four simple indices also prepared for each state in 1960 and 1980.

The general decrease in diversity in the total sample was also reflected in almost all the individual sample states. The Gini index for seven of the eight states was higher in 1980 than in 1960; in the eighth state, which was among the least diverse in both study years, there was a very small decrease in the index. Of the sixteen measurements of diversity taken in the eight states over two different years, six of the eight most diverse ones were from states in 1960.

Three of the Pearson correlation coefficients were quite high and significant at better than the .01 level. The correlation between the Gini index and index A (the number of institutions divided by the number of types) was +.825; the correlation with index C (the percentage of institutions in the first 10 percent of types) was +.876; and the correlation with index D (the percentage of institutions that were singlets) was —.711. Indices A and C in particular appear to be reasonable proxies for diversity as measured by the Gini index when the calculation of the Lorenz curve is not desired. On the other hand, index B (the percentage of institutions in the largest type), while positively (+.530) correlated, was too weakly related to be used for this purpose.

One additional calculation on state data was performed: The factor of size (number of institutions in the state) was used as a variable. The Gini index of each state correlated +.318 with number of institutions, so there was a tendency for diversity in a state to decrease as the number of institutions increased. The tendency was only moderate, and in fact, the most diverse state in 1960 had exactly the same number of institutions as did the least diverse state in 1980. Even so, the positive relationship between the state Gini index and the number of institutions in the state may account for some portion of the decrease in diversity in the total sample between 1960 and 1980. The reasons for this tendency are unclear. Perhaps many of the diversity matrix's cells are so highly improbable that the number of potentially available species is in fact much smaller than that suggested by the total number of matrix cells. Once there are institutions in the most highly probable cells, there then may be a tendency for additional institutions to add to existing cells rather than to be in a sharply different one. On the other hand, the answer may be related to structural or political variables since states with the highest percentage increase in the number of institutions in the base year tended to also have the highest increases in the Gini index.

A third possible explanation is suggested by Blau's (1973) finding that although increasing organizational size increases differentiation, it does so at a decreasing rate. This same principle may operate in systems of organizations as well as in individual organizations. If so, the relationship between the number of institutions and the number of institutional types would be expected to be nonlinear and a large increase in types would not be expected merely because of the large increase in institutions. Certainly, some increase in types would be expected with a large increase in institutions, but this was not seen in this study's sample. The difference between expected and existing types might be caused by nonsignificant fluctuations in the number of types or an asymptotic relationship between the two variables, so that as the number of institutions increases, the number of types first rises rapidly, then rises more slowly, and finally reaches a final value regardless of any increase in the number of institutions. Further research is needed to determine the factors related to these changes.

Changes in Institutional Types

Data in Chapter Five indicated the significant changes that occurred in the several variables describing institutions in the population between 1960 and 1980. These descriptions were all reported in terms of single variables. Now with the identification of institutional types, it is possible to look again at the population and indicate how it changed during that period.

This examination consists of answering two major questions. First, how did the distributions of institutional types compare during the twenty-year period? Answering this question requires examining the extent to which the same types existed during both study years and others existed in one study year but not the next.

Second, what were the major changes in the population by institutional types, and what factors accounted for those changes? The large number of institutional types makes it impractical to answer this question completely. Instead, only the largest institutional types in 1960 and 1980 were compared and changes in their status over the twenty-year period identified.

There were 141 institutional types identified in 1960 and 138 types in 1980. There were ninety types common to both periods, leaving fifty-one types that existed in 1960 but not in 1980 and forty-eight types that existed in 1980 but not in 1960. Some types that had disappeared by 1980 or appeared after 1960 were represented by only a small number of institutions. Whether their development or demise represents the process of natural selection or merely aberrations in the sample is therefore problematic. In other cases, however, the changes in the distribution of types involved a large number of institutions. Table 12 shows the distribution of types that had at least fifteen institutions in either 1960 or 1980. For both years, all institutions shown were nonminority, so this variable has not been identified on the table.

Table 12 has a total of eighteen different, most common institutional types; three of the eight most common types in 1960 were also among the top eight in 1980. The eighteen most common types include institutions representing all control values, all degree-level values, all curriculum values, all size values, and both sex values; no value of any of the variables appears to dominate the list of most frequent institutions in either of the two years.

Although changes in the characteristics of the most common institutional types were not startlingly different between 1960 and 1980, the distributions of types within the total population changed significantly. Within the context of the natural selection model, institutional types that increased their representation within the population can be considered as hav-

Table 12. Types with Fifteen or More Institutions in 1960 or 1980.

Characteristics of Type	*1960* No.	*1960* Rank	*1980* No.	*1980* Rank
Public, two-year, comprehensive, small, coeducational	53	1	27	5
Religious, four-year, liberal arts, small, single-sex	35	2	11	22
Public, two-year, comprehensive, medium, coeducational	24	3	58	2
Public, two-year, teacher ed., small, coeducational	22	4	...	...
Religious, four-year, liberal arts, small, coeducational	18	5	19	9
Religious, two-year, liberal arts, small, single-sex	16	6	...	...
Public, master's, teacher ed., medium, coeducational	15	7	...	...
Independent, master's, professional, small, coeducational	15	8	20	7
Public, two-year, comprehensive, large, coeducational	9	14	123	1
Public, master's, comprehensive, large, coeducational	8	17	47	3
Public, doctor's, comprehensive, large, coeducational	12	10	37	4
Independent, doctor's, comprehensive, large, coeducational	11	11	25	6
Public, two-year, professional, large, coeducational	...	...	19	9
Religious, four-year, liberal arts, medium, coeducational	5	36	19	9
Independent, four-year, professional, small, coeducational	7	22.5	18	11
Proprietary, two-year, professional, small, coeducational	4	46.5	17	12
Independent, two-year, comprehensive, small, coeducational	2	77	15	13.5
Independent, four-year, liberal arts, small, coeducational	5	35.5	15	13.5

ing been positively selected by the environment; those institutional types that were seen less frequently in the population in 1980 can be considered as having been negatively selected.

To evaluate the extent of changes involving enough institutions so that differences were not likely to have been caused by random or unique events, only the effects of selection upon those types that had fifteen or more institutions in at least one of the two study years were analyzed. An institutional type was considered negatively selected if the number of institutions in it dropped by 50 percent between 1960 and 1980; types were identified positively selected if their numbers at least doubled during the same period. In all, there were five negatively and eleven positively selected types in the sample (two additional types were stable during the period).

If natural selection had been the dominant process affecting the survival of institutions and institutional types, it would be expected that institutional failure caused reductions in the number of institutions in a negatively selected type. It is possible, however, that other processes reduced the numbers of institutions of a certain type. Institutions could have changed their programs or their size, for example, and thus prospered in 1980 even though the institutional type in which they were formerly categorized had disappeared. To examine more closely the nature of the changes in the distribution of institutional types, specific changes that had occurred by 1980 are shown for negatively selected institutional types in Table 13 and for positively selected types in Table 14.

Read Table 13 across: Institutional type A had fifty-three institutions in 1960. By 1980, six had failed, twenty-nine had increased in size and so were another type, nine had remained the same, and nine had changed their control, degree level, curriculum, or sex of student body (or some combination) and were in another type. In addition, there were eighteen newly created institutions in this type. The result of all these changes was that the number of institutions in this type had decreased to twenty-seven by 1980.

The data in Table 13 indicate that there were significant differences in the processes by which the number of institutions in the five negatively selected types were reduced. For type C, institutional failure caused the change from twenty-two institutions in 1960 to none in 1980. Institutional failure also primarily reduced type D, although somewhat fewer than a third of the

Table 13. Changes of Negatively Selected Institutional Types Between 1960 and 1980.

Characteristics of Institutional Type	*Total 1960*	*1980 Status of 1960 Institutions*				*Addi-tions*	*Total 1980*
		Failed	*Grew*	*Same*	*Changed*		
A. Public, two-year, comprehensive, small, coeducational	53	6	29	9	9	18	27
B. Religious, four-year, liberal arts, small, single-sex	35	8	1	8	18	3	11
C. Public, two-year, teacher ed., small, coeducational	22	22	0	0	0	0	0
D. Religious, two-year, liberal arts, small, single-sex	16	11	0	0	5	0	0
E. Public, master's, teacher ed., medium, coeducational	15	0	0	0	15	0	0
	141	47	30	17	47	21	38

Table 14. Changes of Positively Selected Institutional Types Between 1960 and 1980.

Characteristics of Institutional Type	Total 1960	Change Since 1960			New	Total 1980
		Grew	Same	Other		
A. Public, two-year, comprehensive, large, coeducational	9	35	5	7	76	123
B. Public, two-year, comprehensive, medium, coeducational	24	13	0	2	43	58
C. Public, master's, large, comprehensive, coeducational	8	3	1	33	10	47
D. Public, doctor's, comprehensive, large, coeducational	12	0	12	20	5	37
E. Independent, doctor's, comprehensive, large, coeducational	11	2	9	11	3	25
F. Public, two-year, professional, large, coeducational	0	6	0	3	10	19
G. Independent, four-year, professional, small, coeducational	7	0	2	4	12	18
H. Religious, four-year, liberal arts, medium, coeducational	5	2	3	11	3	19
I. Proprietary, two-year, professional, small, coeducational	4	0	1	0	16	17
J. Independent, four-year, liberal arts, small, coeducational	5	0	2	5	8	15
K. Independent, two-year, comprehensive, small, coeducational	2	0	0	5	10	15
	87	61	35	101	196	393

institutions in that type in 1960 still existed, in another type, by 1980. For both types C and D, there were no instances of a new institution being created after 1960 that had the characteristics of the type, nor did any previously existing institution change its characteristics to join this type. The changes observed in the population of types C and D appear consistent with the natural selection model.

The pattern of change in type A was quite different. Although its number of institutions dropped from fifty-three in 1960 to twenty-seven in 1980, this reduction was caused primarily by institutional growth rather than institutional failures; a majority of institutions in type A were still in existence in 1980 but had increased their enrollment, thus placing them in another institutional type. The meaning of the changes in type A depends upon the extent to which changes of institutional size can really be considered as the failure of a smaller institution and the creation of a larger one. Agreement with this interpretation would identify type C as consistent with the natural selection model. However, considering growth as the result of strategic policy decisions by institutions would support more clearly the resource dependence model. The fact that eighteen new institutions were added to type A after 1960, while only six actually failed, suggests that the latter position is more supportable, but no firm conclusions are possible.

The patterns of types B and E are much less equivocal. In both cases, their number of institutions dropped dramatically between the two study years. Although a small proportion of the drop of type B can be explained by institutional failure, the most significant differences in type B, and all the differences in type E, occurred because of institutions that survived the twenty-year study period but changed their type regarding control, degree level, curriculum, sex of student body, or some combination of these variables. For types B and E, the resource dependence model appears to explain more reasonably the reductions in the population of an institutional type than does the natural selection approach.

In summary, there were five institutional types whose populations decreased significantly during the twenty-year study period. The changes in types C and D appeared consistent with the concepts of natural selection, types B and E could be explained more readily by the concepts of resource dependence, and type A was equivocal.

While the populations of some institutional types significantly decreased during the twenty-year study period, others grew; Table 14 shows the growth patterns for these types. These data indicate the total number of institutions in eleven positively selected types in 1980 and the component changes since 1960 that led to that number. For example, type A had only 9 institutions in 1960 but had grown to 123 by 1980. Of these 123 schools, 35 existed in 1960 but were smaller then; they grew into this institutional type by 1980. In addition, five institutions were in the same type in both years, seven institutions were in a different institutional type in 1960 and changed their control, program, degree level, or sex of student body by 1980 to enter this type, and seventy-six institutions did not exist in 1960 but were newly created in this institutional type by 1980.

Changes in institutional type consistent with the natural selection model would be reflected by increases in institutions in a type primarily because of replication or the development of new institutions that had the same characteristics of a group that had been positively selected. Six institutional types, A, B, F, G, I, and K in Table 14, follow that pattern. Although in some cases institutions were in these types in 1980 because of growth or changes of other kinds, the largest proportion of the increase of these institutions was due to the creation of new ones that did not exist in 1960.

Viewing institutional change through the lens of the resource dependence model focuses upon changes in the size of types caused primarily by changes in program, degree level, student sex, or control that increased an institution's ability to obtain resources and represented its response to the environment. These changes are the dominant ones in types C, D, E, and H. A third grouping, type J, changed between 1960 and 1980 because of a mixture of new institutions, changes in size, or changes in other characteristics in which none of these changes strongly predominated. For type J, the evidence suggesting the operation of one model or the other is equivocal.

This analysis of the changes of institutional types over

the twenty-year study period can be summarized. Sixteen institutional types had at least fifteen institutions during one or both of the study years, and their numbers had either increased or decreased significantly between 1960 and 1980. If these changes can be explained by using the natural selection model to examine organizational populations, increases in a type are caused primarily by the "birth" of new institutions and decreases by their "death." Eight institutional types did exhibit that pattern. An alternative explanation for organizational change, the resource dependence model, focuses upon institutions' ability to make tactical and strategic choices in response to environmental pressures. This model suggests that changes in organizational populations occur through institutional decisions to change various aspects of their programs and operations. Six of the institutional types did exhibit that pattern of change. The remaining two institutional types showed patterns of change that included mixtures of new institutions, program changes, or changes in size that were not clear enough to justify their placement into either of the two models. The data indicate that over the past twenty years, both the natural selection and resource dependence models contribute to an understanding of the dynamics through which diversity in higher education has changed; a total perspective is incomplete if it considers only one model to the exclusion of the other.

New Directions in Diversity Research

The diversity upon which the higher education system's stability and responsiveness depends was analyzed in the previous chapters primarily from the perspective of the natural selection model of organizational change. The model uses the three-stage process of variation, selection, and retention to explain a major portion of the changes in the population of institutions of higher education over the twenty-year period from 1960 to 1980. The environment within which these institutions exist has various niches—combinations of resources within which institutions exhibiting certain characteristics can compete and survive. Institutional types that locate appropriate niches in which they are the most fit survive and may be replicated within the population; those that do not may decrease in number or disappear altogether, through either institutional failure or loss of identity and incorporation into some other organization.

An analysis of the natural selection of organizations requires the determination of institutional types, which are analogous to biological species. Using six variables related to organizational form and activity, an inclusive and exhaustive identification of all possible institutional types was created through the development of a diversity matrix. All institutions of higher education in existence in 1960 in a sample of eight states were identified, placed into the appropriate cell of the matrix, and tallied. The same process was followed for all institutions existing in 1980. Although there were many more institutions in the sample in 1980 than in 1960, the number of different institutional types in fact slightly decreased during the study period. Lorenz curve analysis was used to assess the differences in the dispersal and concentration of institutions over the twenty-year study period, through the creation of a diversity index. The index was higher for 1980 than for 1960, indicating a decrease in diversity during these two time periods.

This study's findings indicate that to some extent evidence supports both sides of the diversity debate. On the one hand, it is true that American higher education has been, and still is, extremely diverse. There are a large number of different institutional types, and although some types that existed in 1960 are no longer present in the system, new types that themselves did not exist two decades ago have been created. The net result is that there are almost as many different institutional types now as there were in 1960.

On the other hand, during a period of unprecedented growth in American higher education, the number of different institutional types has not increased. From a comparison of the total number of types and institutions during the two study years, the various indices computed indicated that diversity is slowly decreasing. This finding is consistent with the ecological and organizational principles that organisms become more uniform as their environments become more similar and follows the patterns suggested in Chapter Three. It appears that the higher education system has used the vast increase in resources primarily to replicate existing forms (such as the community college) rather than to create new ones.

Given the essential functions that diversity plays in the higher education system, any diminution should be viewed with concern. A responsive system should have the capacity to change, but that capacity is diminished as the number of kinds of institution is reduced. Even in a relatively stable environment, societal needs and interests change, and all the evidence now available indicates that the environment of higher education over the next twenty years will be anything but stable. Projected enrollment declines of traditional students, greater interest in serving nontraditional populations, reduced public priorities for higher education in competition with other compelling social needs, limited fiscal ability of state governments, and increases in cost differentials between public and private institutions are just several of the pressures expected to affect the higher education system. As a consequence, the resources available to the system will decline, environmental forces leading to negative selection will increase, and as institutions fail or merge, the niches they occupy will change.

There are a number of possible scenarios to depict possible changes in the system of higher education in response to this reduction in resources. Two are sufficient to show the range of outcomes. In the first scenario, changing environmental conditions and niches negatively select certain types of institution, and their numbers significantly diminish or disappear. At the same time, new institutional forms are created, some of which will be able to prosper within the new niches and become more important elements in the population over the next twenty years. Although the number of *institutions* will decrease (this is a probable but by no means necessary outcome of diminished enrollments), the number of *kinds* of institution will remain unchanged or perhaps even grow. The level of diversity will thus be maintained, and institutional variation in the year 2000 will be great enough to respond to the changing environment of the following twenty years.

The second scenario begins, as did the first, with the negative selection of institutional types in the face of environmental pressures. Instead of new institutional types to meet the demands of the new niches being created, however, existing institutions will compete with one another by expanding into them. As a consequence, by the year 2000, diversity will have decreased; there will be fewer institutional types, and institutions will look more and more alike. As new needs arise during the first two decades of the twenty-first century, there will be fewer variations within the population that could be used to respond.

The data in this study suggest that at present the second scenario is more probable than the first for American higher education. It is also more dangerous. In general, one major source of variation in organizational populations has been the founding of new organizations (Aldrich and Pfeffer, 1976). This is certainly true of higher education, and in the past it was through the development of such new forms that the system remained responsive. Constraints to the development of such new forms over the next twenty years could profoundly affect the vitality and viability of the entire system of colleges and universities.

The diversity index offers policy analysts and other researchers a stable and objective means for quantitatively assessing the level of diversity as it exists in different locations and during different time periods. It is possible to consider the diversity index as either a dependent or an independent variable in policy research. As a dependent variable, the index can be used to study the effects of certain policies upon institutional diversity at national, regional, or state levels. As an independent variable, the index can be used to examine the effect of levels of diversity upon other critical policy variables. Several examples of each variable illustrate the possibilities; for our purposes, the geographical unit of analysis is the state, although for various purposes other regional units could be used.

The Index as a Dependent Variable. Each of the fifty states have somewhat different structures and policies for coordinating or governing institutions of higher education. Typologies have been established that permit grouping states based upon the general form of the statewide coordinating system. No intensive studies of the relative effectiveness of various forms of state governance systems have been done (Mortimer and McConnell, 1978). Although there are many dimensions to the concept of effectiveness, certainly one must be the provision of diversity. To what extent is diversity related to statewide organizational form? Do changes in governance form appear related to changes in levels of diversity? If so, over what time period do such changes take place? Hannan and Freeman (1977) suggested the examination of the impact of variables of state regulation upon diversity of organizational forms such as colleges and universities as one means of assessing the validity of the natural selection model.

Various states have established programs whose avowed intention is the provision of assistance to the nonpublic sector. Are states with such programs more or less diverse than states without them? Do such programs appear to increase diversity over time? Maintain present levels? Decelerate rates of decrease? Policies regarding the extent to which nonpublic institutions are subject to state-level review of academic program and other aspects of institutional functioning differ from state to state. In addition, the depth of such review, and the authority of the state to take action subsequent to it, vary considerably. To what extent are such state policies related to diversity?

The Index as an Independent Variable. Since diversity is an indication of responsiveness to different environmental pressures, such as student interest, perhaps diversity is related to attendance patterns. To what extent is diversity related to the proportion of a state's high school graduates who continue their education? To the proportion of high school graduates who migrate to other states?

Is a state's degree of diversity related to the attendance of various categories of students? Minority students? Adult learners?

Other Research Questions. At least two types of research directions usefully continue the focus of our analysis. The first concerns the variables that define an institutional type. It has been noted already that although the variables used in this study have a certain face validity, other variables could have been selected. The number of variables and their values significantly affect the number of types defined, and although the Gini index appears relatively stable, it is not certain that it would remain so when different variables are manipulated. A major cause for concern in the present study is the large number of singlets, perhaps indicating that some of the variables used in defining categories are related more to subspecies than species. Further effort is needed to determine the validity of the definitions used here and to propose more appropriate ones if necessary. A first step might be to compare the institutional types found here with other typologies, such as the revised Carnegie classification. Another alternative is the use of more sophisticated statistical techniques, such as cluster analysis or discriminant analysis, to attempt to identify types. Pursuing this question is important for further study of the processes by which colleges and universities interact with their environments, but it will prove to be an exceptionally difficult undertaking. Aldrich's (1979) review of the empirical literature on organization-environment interaction indicated that most research has focused upon adaptation rather than selection. In addition, in the absence of "any agreed-upon criteria for identifying qualitative breaks between organizational forms" (p. 110), it is difficult to state with any assurance whether differences in organizations represent new organizational forms or merely new adaptations within similar forms.

A second type of research direction uses the concept of institutional type to identify groups of institutions comparable on five of the six variables and then to gather additional information about these institutions to gain further insight into the issue of diversity. For example, it often has been suggested, but never empirically demonstrated, that the nonpublic sector serves an important function by permitting the development of innovations and new programs not possible in public institutions. Catalogue reviews of, for example, medium-sized, comprehensive, four-year, coeducational, nonminority institutions that are public with nonpublic ones would permit the collection of data with which to test that belief.

Similarly, a comparison of catalogue and other information over time could be useful for assessing to an even finer degree the extent to which diversity is increasing or decreasing. By looking at the same institutional type in 1960 and 1980, variables in addition to the ones used in this study could be compared to see whether variation has decreased within as well as between types. Variables to be examined (which would require collection of additional data not possible in this study) might include the proportion of students in residence halls, selectivity, distribution of minority and nonminority students, proportion of older students, proportion of students in graduate programs, and similar measures. The purpose of such analyses would be to determine if institutions of the same type are more or less different now than they were in the past.

It would be desirable also to collect data for the 1960–1980 time period for additional states and to expand the time period by examining documentation from 1950, and, to the extent available, 1940 as well. A long time span is required to apply appropriately the principles of population ecology to the study of organizations (Aldrich and Pfeffer, 1976). Placing the data within a longer time frame can indicate the extent to which changes are minor perturbations or part of a long-term trend.

This study may help redirect some research attention from the role of leadership toward a better understanding of the environment's effect upon colleges and universities. A ubiquitous theme in the literature of institutional survival is that of a strong leader, buttressed by elaborate planning systems and strategic marketing practices (for example, see Mayhew, 1979). Institutional demise, on the other hand, is treated as the equivalent of administrative weakness, the failure to search for new markets, and the inability to forecast future needs. The purpose here is not to belittle the importance of skillful administration or the art of exploiting new demands through strategic planning but to point out that the often-mentioned strategies may be functional only for those institutions that have been selected for retention for reasons other than the enterprising nature of their administrators. Unfortunately, there is no empirical evidence or qualitative studies of institutions to support this argument.

7

Recommendations for Maintaining Diversity

This study focused upon the value of diversity and noted a decline in the level of institutional diversity with concern but not alarm. This chapter suggests several steps that might be taken to preserve and perhaps even enhance the future level of diversity in this country's higher education system. In doing so, it is recognized that diversity has costs as well as benefits and is only one value among many that policy makers must consider. Among the costs are the difficulty of developing within the system any recognized reference points that can be used to measure quality, the failure to make it possible to identify any common characteristics of a college education, the impossibility of rationalizing the system, the persistence of institutional inequalities and consequent inequalities in the level of services offered to students, and the high fiscal cost of supporting a system with so much built-in slack. Policy makers who have major influence upon the allocation of resources must balance many values, and they cannot afford (either financially or politically) to make the optimization of diversity their primary goal. At the same time, in the past, perhaps diversity was not given the attention it deserved in discussions of public policy. It is hoped that at least to some extent this study will help correct that imbalance. The proper perspective is the one Trow (1979, p. 289) offered:

> Any principle can become a dogma, a substitute for judgment rather than a guide and touchstone for decision making. The principle of diversity can more properly enter academic decisions as a counterweight to short-term and narrow conceptions of academic efficiency. And it can remind administrators and planners of the irony of functional adaptation, an irony known to students of biological evolution, that short-term efficiency associated with highly successful adaptation to present circumstances may be maladaptive to the future. Conversely, a degree of organizational complexity that is "inefficient" in the short run may prove more adaptive to unforeseen problems and opportunities, demands and pressures that lie ahead. The lesson, implicit in the whole history of American higher education, has to be learned anew in every generation.

To a great extent, the usefulness of any model is a function of its ability to offer new perspectives in which phenomena may be seen and analyzed. The natural selection approach leads to statements in support of diversity, which in many cases are not dissimilar from conventional wisdom. The analysis that supports these conclusions, however, based upon variability as an essential requirement to ensure the stability and environmental responsiveness of an ecological system, gives new insight into *why* diversity is important and suggests several consequences of reducing diversity.

Over the next twenty years, there should be significant changes in the population of this country's higher education system as competition for increasingly scarce resources intensifies. Most likely this competition will lead to a reduction of diversity as measured by the diversity index, thus continuing the trend of the last twenty years. The consequences could have profound implications for the higher education system specifically and for American society in general. What insights does the natural selection model provide concerning policies that would tend to increase diversity? This chapter provides some answers to that question.

Encouraging Variation

There are two kinds of variability in institutions of higher education: a diversity of institutional types (species) and different approaches to problems in institutions of the same type (genetic variability). Although many environmental forces tend to make institutions similar to one another in many respects, certain other environmental pressures specific to individual niches can cause changes in institutions and their populations if the processes of natural selection are permitted to function.

System responsiveness and stability are strengthened by permitting and indeed encouraging new structures and programs in higher education. As Weick (1979) pointed out, only if a variation has appeared once is it available for selection. Although the desirability of such diversity and variation enjoys general rhetorical support, accomplishing it is often exceptionally difficult. This is particularly true in public systems of higher education, and it may also be true among private institutions that require comprehensive state review for approval of new institutions or new programs.

There are several ways diversity and variability could be encouraged in such situations. First, states could temper their understandable concern for quality with an enhanced appreciation of the values of diversity. In some states, the establishment of quantitative and qualitative standards for licensing or other approval of nonpublic institutions serves several important functions but at the same time is apt to focus upon traditional criteria, such as the number of faculty with graduate degrees. This definition of quality assumes a consensus concerning the purposes of higher education that is by no means universal.

The dual purpose of ensuring quality while promoting diversity might be satisfied by creating two alternative levels of state review against which newly created institutions, or those being reevaluated, would be judged, rather than one. The first level, perhaps called registration, would signify that the institution was in compliance with state health and safety laws, its materials and advertising were not misleading, and it was not operating in an educationally or fiscally fraudulent manner. Registration would not imply state endorsement or approval of the institution's quality.

A second level of review, perhaps called accreditation, would, at an institution's request, evaluate the school against a set of qualitative and quantitative standards. The granting of accredited status would indicate that the institution met the stated criteria. Should state support be made available, it could be limited to accredited institutions and their students.

Increased activity by the state to disseminate comparative information about campuses to potential clienteles, provide informational counseling, or otherwise publicize the nature of the two-tier evaluation system would enhance diversity by making consumers more knowledgeable and the marketplace more responsive. In addition, each institution could be required to print in its catalogue a state-prepared notice indicating the criteria and procedures for institutional evaluation and its individual status. These steps would enable individuals to make more informed choices, protect the state's interest in guarding quality, and make available to those persons for whom the number of books in the library or the quality of laboratories is not important educational programs of their choosing.

As a second means of increasing diversity, rigid criteria and complex approval processes for new programs could be significantly relaxed. Except for situations in which decisions by one institution involving a high-cost program with a limited pool of potential students and faculty might significantly affect another school, program approval at the undergraduate level should be a matter of institutional, not state, concern. At the very least, some states' current practice of requiring institutions of unquestioned quality and academic integrity to submit to the state detailed proposals for approval of common undergraduate curricula should be abandoned. The question of program control and review at the graduate level is more problematic because many of the institutions relate to national or regional rather than local markets and often involve professional licensing standards. State concern in such areas is reasonable, and intrusive program-review procedures may be justified in such cases.

Under a two-tiered rating system, there would be no need for regular evaluation of programs at registered campuses. Potential program-quality problems in accredited institutions could be dealt with through periodic post hoc reviews rather than preapproval evaluations. Even this should be done with caution, however. If the state's criteria are too limited, "qualitative reassessments of the needs, functions, and social objectives of postsecondary education in [a] state . . . could even indicate that some institutions or programs no longer serve any important function and thus are qualitatively irrelevant" (Education Commission of the States, 1980, p. 24). To protect diversity, it would be better for the marketplace rather than the state to make such decisions. Great caution should be exercised to prevent premature assessment or attempts to close programs considered "undesirable" or "weak" by contemporary standards, except in the case of fraud.

Third, greater flexibility than now exists in many states could be allowed public institutions in their administrative, fiscal, and program-development processes. Some states' elaborate systems to ensure accountability and prevent "error" also limit variety because of the likelihood that they will standardize the institutions under their control (Mortimer and McConnell, 1978). Using formula rather than line-item budgeting, following post- rather than preaudit accounting procedures, and providing institutional autonomy in such areas as purchasing and personnel have been widely recommended ways of increasing institutional flexibility. However, these means also create the institutional differences that, if natural selection is allowed to function, protect the system as well.

Diversity in public systems could be further enhanced by changing the kinds of limitations statewide or system master plans often place upon institutional development. By often prescribing completely an institution's academic program, enrollment size, potential constituents, and other critical dimensions of institutional diversity, the plans limit these institutions' responsiveness to changing environments. One simple change would give institutions greater opportunity to experiment with new structures: Write mission statements regarding what institutions could *not* do rather than what they *must* do. Within these constraints, institutions could be free to respond to the environment as they wished, with fixed budget parameters and the expressed interests of potential constituents over time providing the selection pressures necessary for evolution.

It is likely that as resources become scarcer over the next two decades, state governments will become even more directive than they are now, to remain cost-effective. This centralization of academic power is a serious threat to diversity (Trow, 1979). The natural selection perspective suggests that long-term cost-effectiveness would be better served by decreasing, rather than increasing, state control.

At the same time that the state should be concerned about minimizing present barriers to future diversity and variability, it should be certain that it not take actions that, in the absence of any compelling public policy to the contrary, would reduce the existing diversity. For example, although public policy regarding discrimination clearly would be more compelling than any advantage of increasing diversity by permitting all-white colleges to practice discrimination by race, the same claim does not apply to predominantly black (or other minority) institutions. Such institutions contribute to institutional diversity in this country, and as long as they continue to attract a constituency (which, by the way, has always included nonminority students), attempts by the federal government to integrate them should be resisted.

The greatest challenges of the next twenty years may not be how to remain cost-effective during a period of decline but how to maintain the requisite variety of a responsive system and encourage change. "Just as most biological mutations are regressive, or at least non-viable, change is not always for the better; often it is for the worse. But the difficulty of change in higher education, as in the biological world, would reduce adaptability to new circumstances and the chances for improvement even if circumstances do not change. Thus, it is important that opportunities for new developments be kept open even in a period when growth no longer provides an easy opening for their introduction" (Carnegie Foundation, 1976, p. 7).

Maintaining Ecological Pressure and Differential Constraints

Complex systems, whether biological or social, are maintained by constant ecological pressures (Campbell, 1969). Two factors tend to degrade such systems in the absence of this pressure of selective retention. One factor is that variations introduced into the system and not made vulnerable to retention processes reduce the system's functionality. The other factor is that systems tend to move toward simplicity and standardization to stabilize their activities (Aldrich, 1979). The consequence of these two tendencies is to move systems to a simpler and less organized state and to remove deviants and encourage a uniform outlook by system members.

This country's present system of higher education is complex because of environmental pressures. Removing such pressures will make it less complex and therefore less responsive. This suggests that heroic efforts to preserve individual institutions unable to find niches in which they can successfully compete, although proposed in the name of saving diversity, in the long term might have exactly the opposite effect. Not only will this attempt preserve forms no longer environmentally fit, it will prevent other, perhaps more suitable forms, from evolving and moving into a vacant niche. An ecological perspective suggests that in a complex and interdependent system, short-term but expedient solutions ultimately may have long-term and undesirable consequences.

This means that public funds should not be used to "bail out" private institutions unable to maintain fiscally sound enrollment bases, nor should public systems maintain through special budget allocations low-demand public colleges that are no longer competitive. The issue is not the survival of individual institutions but the maintenance of a responsive system. As Finn (1978, p. 220) said, "The health of those institutions that happen to exist in 1978 should not be equated with the well-being of higher education as a whole. The preservationist approach is tempting; it is usually easier in public policy deliberations to argue for freezing the status quo than to define, and win, converts to any formula for changing it. Yet there is no reason to assume that the three thousand colleges and universities in existence today are the ones the nation will need ten or twenty years hence, and there is ample reason to resist policy formulations meant to keep them as they are."

Factors other than budget also constrain institutions' development and evolution, including social, political, organizational, legal, and other considerations, many of which were discussed in Chapter Two as factors that limit the strategic policy choices of institutions.

Based upon earlier comments concerning the need to increase institutional opportunities for diversity and internal variation, it might be thought that diversity would increase if these constraints upon institutional decisions were eliminated. However, this would not be true. The constraints upon an organization define what is possible for that institution, and by doing so, they also set the boundaries of its niche (Zammuto, 1982). These constraints make certain responses to the environment more probable than other responses (Pfeffer and Salancik, 1978) and account for the differences in institutional types. As constraints in the higher education system decrease or become more uniform, diversity of institutions would be expected to decrease. On the other hand, increasing constraints increases the upper bounds of diversity (Hannan and Freeman, 1977).

The critical aspect of constraints is that to increase diversity they must be distinct and heterogeneous across institutional types. This is why having different institutions subject to different state laws, different regional and professional accrediting associations, different funding mechanisms, pressures from different social or political groups, and differing on each of the other constraints now operating in the system at a local level maintains and protects diversity. It was pointed out that "the expansion of markets and state control mechanisms through social systems tends to have the consequence of eliminating or reducing the number of constraints which are idiosyncratic to local environments" (Hannan and Freeman, 1977, p. 944). When local constraints are replaced by more uniform ones set at state or national levels, the effect will be a reduction in diversity, which is one reason why proposals for establishing national accrediting standards, for example, should be resisted, and why attempts to increase the purview of state coordinating boards are likely to lead to a more simplified, and therefore a more vulnerable, system.

The implication of the necessity for differential constraints is that the marketplace itself cannot be the only controlling force if diversity is to survive. In the absence of constraints, institutional roles will converge rather than differentiate (Clark, 1981), and diversity will be reduced significantly.

Competition and Competitive Exclusion

Hannan and Freeman (1977) said that "Organizational forms presumably fail to flourish in certain environmental circumstances because other forms successfully compete with them for essential resources. As long as the resources which sustain organizations are finite and populations have unlimited capacity to expand, competition must ensue" (p. 940).

It can be argued that during the decade of the 1960s and at least the first years of the 1970s, the conditions for competition, at least systemwide, did not exist. Resources, while obviously not infinite, in most cases were available at a level sufficient to meet the needs and ambitions of most institutions, and there seemed to be no limit to the extent to which expansion of the population could be supported. Increasingly during the next twenty years the resources available to higher education will be finite and not great enough to support all existing members of the population (at least not at their present sizes). Competition is expected to become an increasingly important part of institutional and system life during this future period.

Chapter One mentioned that in biology the functioning of natural selection at the species level is reflected in the principle of competitive exclusion, which states that two or more species cannot achieve a stable balance when they attempt to fill the same role in the same community (Whittaker and Levin, 1975). That is, if resources are limited, no two species can occupy the same niche. The same principle can be applied to organizations: "If two populations or organizations sustained by identical environmental resources differ in some organizational characteristic, that population with the characteristic less fit to environmental contingencies will tend to be eliminated" (Hannan and Freeman, 1977, p. 943).

Note that the concept of competition among higher education institutions does not mean that all institutions will be competing with one another. Instead, it suggests that the competition will occur between institutions that attempt to secure the same resources and that therefore attempt to occupy the same niche. The religiously controlled liberal arts college and the public comprehensive community college may be across the street from each other, but because they occupy different niches and draw upon different resources, they will not be in competition. However, the same may not be said about the regional state university and the nonselective comprehensive independent institution that draw similar students from a common geographical area. The principle of competitive exclusion indicates that without constraints, only one of these institutional types will be able to survive.

The ultimate outcome of the operation of the principle upon institutions attempting to fill the same niche will be a reduction in diversity. This outcome can be forestalled two ways. One is to permit the institutions to continue to occupy the same niche but to establish differential constraints upon them, which prevent the stronger from driving out the weaker. Constraints might be mandated limits upon enrollment (that is, specifying that schools may be able to acquire only a certain portion of the available resources), limitations upon program offerings, or some other management device. Alternatively, one of the institutions could alter the pattern of resources upon which it depends, by either creating a new niche for itself or identifying an available but empty niche into which it could move.

In the "worse-case" situation, institutions attempting to change their niches would be precluded from doing so by the inflexible policies of external agencies and thus would have to engage in direct competition. In biology, evolution in directions that *reduce* competition is the major source of species diversity (Whittaker and Levin, 1975). Permitting competition without at the same time offering opportunities for selection of new niches therefore reduces the complexity of the system and decreases diversity.

Generalize or Specialize: The Dilemma of Institutional Survival

Biological organisms as well as organizations can be either specialists or generalists. Specialists in higher education include institutions that offer programs attractive only to students with certain religious beliefs, admit only men or only women, or offer a limited range of programs, and other institutions that significantly limit the potential constituency from which they can obtain their resources. Specialists occupy a comparatively narrow niche. Generalists in higher education, on the other hand, offer a wide range of programs and services to a more varied potential constituency and occupy a comparatively broad niche.

Within limits, institutions have the ability to choose whether they will specialize or generalize. Both alternatives have certain attractions. Specialists outcompete generalists over the range of outcomes to which they have become specialized (Hannan and Freeman, 1977). Liberal arts colleges, for example, should be more effective in producing the outcomes associated with that kind of program than a general, comprehensive institution whose liberal arts programs are only one aspect of the college's curriculum. Liberal arts colleges are able to do so because they can focus upon a small set of specific activities and structures and do not have to maintain the additional resources, or "slack," general organizations that have to constantly shift between programs need. Specialization also has costs; generally, adaptation decreases adaptability (Zammuto, 1982), and as organizations become more specialized, they are less able to change to respond to new circumstances and environmental pressures.

Institutional generalists also have positive and negative outcomes to consider. They can spread their fitness over a greater variety of environmental states, thus adapting to changing conditions more rapidly and effectively than can specialists. Doing so, however, requires that organizational resources be kept available for managing such changes; therefore, the resources are not available for supporting the current program.

Specialization or generalization is thus a major factor in the natural selection of colleges and universities, and institutions are responding to the dilemma in various ways. Some are attempting to increase their potential resources and constituencies by changing from a liberal arts to a comprehensive program, removing their religious affiliations, changing admission standards, developing programs that meet the needs of the new students, and otherwise trying to become more general and therefore more attractive to a wider base of students and other supporters. This might appear to be a logical response to the projected changes in the nature of the potential student body over the next twenty years, but it has been suggested that this movement toward generalization, while potentially having short-term positive effects, might be destructive in the long term. Anderson (1977), for example, argued that specialized institutions choosing to generalize will lose the unique characteristics now attracting students and find future recruiting even more difficult. This will be particularly true, he believed, for private institutions, which will be competing unsuccessfully with less expensive public institutions offering similar programs.

Increased generalization also may be destructive to the system by making it less functional. Arguing that some activities are best performed in specialized environments, the Carnegie Commission (1973b) stated that "differentiation of structures can better lead to differentiation of treatment than can the combination of all functions within a single structure" (p. 73). Different functions, they state, therefore can be performed more effectively in different and more specialized kinds of institutions.

Will specialization or generalization confer the greatest ecological advantage over the next twenty years? Although experienced observers have suggested that specialization will increase the chances for institutional survival in the 1980s (Mayhew, 1979), the natural selection model indicates that the question can be answered only by first examining the environment in which the population of institutions exists. In doing so, it should be remembered that although it is possible to refer to the "environment of higher education," in fact, the environment of every institutional type is somewhat different from that of the others (indeed, the isomorphism of environments and species indicates that there are different institutional types precisely *because* their environments are different).

Two major aspects of the environment are critical for understanding the specialization-generalization problem: stability and grain. Stability is the extent to which an environment changes from one state to another. A situation in which the available resource base constantly changed would be unstable. Grain is the degree to which an organism encounters different environmental conditions during its lifetime (Levins, 1968). Environmental variation can be either fine-grained, indicating that an organism will be exposed to many different short-term conditions over its lifetime, or coarse-grained, whereby the organism is faced with significant, long-term differences in environment (Aldrich, 1979; Hannan and Freeman, 1977). The stability of the environment and the characteristics of its grain determine the most effective selection strategy for organizations. Following is a discussion of several examples of optimal strategies for institutions applied to three kinds of environments: stable, unstable and fine-grained, and unstable and coarse-grained.

Stable Environments. Even in the midst of a general decline in resources, some institutions' environments will remain essentially stable or will be likely to change only within a narrow range. For such institutions, specialization will confer a competitive advantage. Institutions that serve a particular and stable clientele based upon similar religious beliefs, unusual mission, selectivity, specialized program, or other unique characteristics therefore would find it advantageous to maintain these distinctions.

Because of their specialized nature, such institutions should be able to compete effectively with more comprehensive institutions offering ostensibly similar programs. Despite this, there may be powerful pressures to expand their mission. Even a stable environment is characterized by minor fluctuations, that, in large institutions, go unnoticed. But specialized institutions are small and therefore vulnerable to such random perturbations. This concern may lead some specialized institutions to explore new student markets that promise to increase or at least maintain enrollments, but because doing so will reduce specialization, it is a self-defeating strategy. Such institutions should utilize their resources to deal more effectively with their present clientele rather than seek new missions.

There are three ways specialized institutions can accomplish this goal. First, there should be increased attention to recruiting. Broad dissemination of information, participation in college nights, or preparation of professionally produced literature are not a good investment for such institutions, however, since their potential market is extremely limited and requires a much more focused approach. The integration of existing students, alumni, and college personnel into a coordinated program of identifying potential applicants is a more effective way of prescreening candidates and making them aware of an institution that shares their interests and values. Second, there should be more attention to following up applicants, to increase the probability that they will enroll. Once a pool of students whose backgrounds make them reasonable candidates for admission has been identified, activities designed to encourage such candidates' enrollment are likely to be more cost-effective than using these same resources to further increase the number of applicants. Third, there should be greater attention to establishing programs designed to reduce attrition. Such programs have been developed in a number of institutions and found effective (Kemerer, Baldridge, and Green, 1982). The obvious purpose of each recommendation is to focus upon recruiting, enrolling, and retaining students whose values are consistent with the institution's specialized mission rather than seeking new sources of students that may compromise the mission.

Even in the 1980s, some specialized institutions may find themselves in the luxurious position of having an abundance of resources. The availability of more qualified applicants than they can accept, budget surpluses, a sound reputation, and other resources that guarantee their stability can be a seductive incitement to grow. It would be wise for such institutions to remain small, however, not only to ensure that they do not outstrip their resource base but to prevent the organizational complexity that comes with increased size and tends to compromise specialization.

Stable environments and consequent specialization have implications for organization, administration, and governance. For instance, specialized institutions have less concern for staffing flexibility than others and would be less likely to use large numbers of adjuncts. They need not pay unusual attention to planning; they could focus upon prudently managing existing resources. General consensus on mission, small size, and simple structure suggests that administration and governance could be more centralized without negatively affecting institutional performance.

Finally, specialized institutions are dependent upon satisfying the needs of a particular constituency. Formal and continuous links with this constituency are critical, both to ensure that the institutions' program meets whatever this group considers criteria of "quality" and to immediately sense any changes in this constituency that makes up the schools' major environmental element.

Unstable, Fine-Grained Environments. In unstable, fine-grained environments, resource availability is likely to shift between states, but the shifts will be reasonably rapid.

Higher education commonly experiences cyclical changes of this type, particularly student interest in enrolling in certain professional areas, such as engineering, business, or education. These cycles may be caused partly by the employment marketplace's response to increased enrollments in an area, leading sequentially after a short delay to increased graduates, decreased job opportunities, decreased enrollments, and new shortages in the field. Freeman (1976) identified this system of enrollment-job market interaction as a classic example of "cobweb dynamics"; these fluctuations can create a fine-grained, unstable environment for some institutions. Similar kinds of market dynamics, although noneconomic, may account for changes in social values, creating cycles in which concern for career preparation gives way after a relatively brief period to reemphasis on the liberal arts, demands for coeducation or integration are superceded by a rediscovery of the value of women's colleges or predominantly black institutions, or personal-development goals yield to a focus upon the basic skills.

In addition to these economic and social factors, environmental fluctuations may be related to demographical trends, such as the decline in the traditional college-age cohort. It is important to remember, however, that even this movement is part of a cyclical trend and that total college enrollments are expected to increase by 1997 (Carnegie Council, 1980), less than fifteen years from this writing. To the extent that these fluctuations are fine-grained changes—changes that will tend to fluctuate over relatively short periods—the optimal institutional strategy again is to specialize. Institutions attempting to respond to each change by being generalists would have to spend most of their time constantly changing their form and structure, thus reducing the resources available for operating the program. Hannan and Freeman (1977) suggested that, under such conditions, it is better to "adopt a specialized structure and 'ride out' the adverse environments" (p. 953).

To do so, institutions should follow the same kind of recruiting and retention recommendations offered to specialized institutions in stable environments. However, optimal administrative and management directions will differ. For example, in an unstable, fine-grained environment, institutions must pay particular attention to staffing flexibility and planning issues. Because the organizations are likely to face frequent environmental changes cyclically, planning how institutional functioning will be adjusted during lean times and periods of prosperity should be an essential and ongoing organizational process. There should be particular attention to establishing a mix of core and adjunct faculty that anticipates and permits relatively rapid shifts in staff components without undue trauma.

One major function of this kind of planning is to preserve the organizational "memory," so that when institutions are in a period of surplus resources, they do not overcommit themselves. Since the tenure of most college presidents is likely to be shorter than the cyclical periods of fine-grained environments, there may be a tendency in the midst of plenty to forget lessons of the past and incorrectly interpret short-term success as a signal for long-term development and growth.

Instead, periods of abundant resources should be used as an opportunity for qualitative improvement that will offer a competitive advantage when environmental changes are encountered and resources become scarce. At the same time, modest enrollment increases, recognized as temporary and requiring only marginal additional costs, can help build up fiscal reserves that can be a buffer against leaner times. Institutions in unstable, fine-grained environments should resist the tendency of most higher education institutions to annually expend their income. More than other institutions, such schools need to prudently plan management of resources in a manner that permits surpluses earned during good times to be balanced against possible deficits in bad times to maintain a reasonably stable internal operation.

These principles hold true for both public and nonpublic institutions, but public colleges face a particular challenge. Their economic situation may be related more to changes of leadership in the statehouse and legislature than to student interests or economic conditions. Public specialized institutions may find it unusually difficult to maintain their specializations during lean times because of enrollment-driven funding formulas and the requirement that funds be spent in the year for which they were appropriated. Diversity in the public sector could be enhanced by permitting institutions to retain funds unspent in one year because of sound management or creative planning and to have them accessible in future years to support program needs during less munificent times. This condition of course would have to be coupled with the level of management and fiscal autonomy already recommended and a "maintenance of effort" mechanism to prevent future legislatures from reducing appropriations because of "surpluses."

Coarse-Grained Environments. In a coarse-grained environment, changes do not regularly fluctuate but are expected to be long-term. In this case, the optimum strategy is to generalize because while the fluctuations in fine-grained environments occur often enough so that specialized institutions can "average them out," in coarse-grained environments, the periods of non-adaptation are long enough to threaten the specialized types. Generalists, on the other hand, will survive, although they will be able to do so inefficiently and by carrying a great deal of organizational slack (Aldrich, 1979). In his study of 2,700 colleges and universities, Zammuto (1983b) confirmed that generalized institutions have been more stable than specialized ones during the past decade.

The best strategy for dealing with coarse-grained environments is to create generalized institutions consisting of specialized and loosely coupled subunits. This strategy, which is generally available only to large institutions, permits organizations to exploit the environment regardless of its state by emphasizing those subunits that happen to enjoy optimal fit at any specific time. Seen in this context, the loose coupling that has led to characterizing colleges and universities as organized anarchies and that so disturbs higher education critics is not an aberration but a structure that the environment has selected as most fit.

This means that the administrative and managerial needs of institutions in coarse-grained environments are much different from those of schools in other settings. Their fitness depends upon having the resources and flexibility to exploit whatever opportunities present themselves. Long-range planning would be of little use, so efforts would be invested more usefully in short-term strategic planning, with particular attention to environmental surveillance. Recruitment should be broadly based rather than focused; concern for student retention is likely to be significantly circumscribed by the availability of new and different clienteles to replace them.

Generalist institutions should have decentralized management structures, permitting relatively autonomous subunits to determine their own survival strategies and isolating failing units so that they do not negatively affect the institution as a whole. To an unusual extent, these institutions must pay attention to the issue of staffing flexibility since their program mix may change radically in response to environmental demands. Although there may be a core program whose activities and personnel are relatively inviolate, generalization requires the ability to reduce or even eliminate other programs that at any given time prove environmentally unfit. This means placing greater reliance upon adjuncts, initiating programs for faculty retraining and relocation, or even considering modifications to the tenure system itself.

Responses of the System. The generalist strategy of specialized but loosely coupled subunits applies to both specific institutional types and the entire population of colleges and universities. If the entire system attempts to generalize, it loses fitness; if it attempts to specialize, it is either inefficient or nonadaptive as the environment changes states. The dilemma in higher education is nicely captured by Clark's (1978) description of the "hazard of the specialized niche in the ecology of similar organizations" (p. 5). Although generalization is a way of hedging bets against sudden changes in the environment, specialization and distinctiveness reduce flexibility and may provide for "rigidity in competence."

Levins (1968) suggested that a biological population's most effective response to the dilemma is polymorphism—the development of populations consisting of specialists in various environments. "The suggestion is that populations combine types . . . some of which are specialized to state 1 and some to state 2. With such a combination at least a portion of the population will always flourish and maintain the genetic diversity which allows it to continue to flourish when the environment changes stage" (Hannan and Freeman, 1977, p. 953). For higher education, polymorphism means that the stability of the system over the long term depends upon the population having available institutions that both specialize (particularly adapted during periods of environmental stability and when the environment is unstable and fine-grained) and generalize (most effective during periods of coarse-grained instability).

The optimal advantages of polymorphism are an additional argument for the desirability of maintaining both strong public and private sectors. The political pressures confronting public institutions require the schools to meet many competing needs and therefore, for the most part, to be generalists (which is one reason why there are almost no public liberal arts colleges). The ability to specialize is therefore primarily located in the private sector. This combination of specialists and generalists is best able to respond to environmental changes affecting the entire system.

Institutions contemplating their specialization-generalization strategy must consider both their own program and the probable state of their future environments before making such decisions. This obviously is not an easy task. Even though ecological theory suggests optimal strategies, there is no easy way to predict in all cases the texture of the environment or even, in the absence of a definition of an organizational "generation," what the dimensions of long- or short-term really are. In addition, strategies that are optimum for a species, or institutional type, do not guarantee the survival of every member of that type.

The Utility of Waste

The preceding section suggested that efficiency, adaptability, and the environment are all interrelated. Specialized institutions can be efficient, but at the cost of being less adaptable. Generalized institutions can be adaptable, but at the cost of being inefficient. A system that evolves through natural selection can optimize both efficiency and effectiveness by maintaining a diversity of types, including both specialized and generalized institutions. This statement has implications for both the higher education system and the management of certain institutions within that system. The message in both cases is the same: To ensure stability and responsiveness, a certain degree of waste is not only inevitable but absolutely essential.

At the system level, there may be a tendency to observe institutions that are struggling to attract students and other resources, that have a program not consistent with contemporary trends or values, or that are engaged in processes or programs at variance with generally accepted norms of quality as being unnecessary or expendable. According to this view, such institutions are wasteful; there is no reason to preserve them, and in fact, they harm the system by diluting an already pressed resource base.

It should be remembered, however, that such judgments can be made only by using contemporary standards, which themselves have been positively selected by past and present environments. The judgments cannot consider the extent to which the programs, policies, procedures, values, or other characteristics preserved by such "wasteful" institutions now might be of value in the future. It is the system's heterogeneity—its essential diversity—that provides for such institutions shelters in which they can survive. Arguing for the need to preserve ideas, forms of organizations, types of persons, and other human artifacts whose current value to the system is unknown, Boulding (1981) said that "This is important in general evolutionary theory because the existence of these heterogeneities and shelters increases the variety of the total gene pool, which may affect the ultimate history of the evolutionary process. When conditions become more favorable outside the shelter, a sheltered species may emerge and occupy a larger habitat" (p. 33).

The system also has a vested interest in protecting apparent waste and inefficiency because of the environment's probabilistic nature. The ultimate tragedy would be guessing that the environment will be either stable or unstable and, after adjusting institutions to be most effective given the projected environment, discovering that the guess was inaccurate. A better gamble is to create different institutional types, each able to function best in a specific environmental state. The cost of doing so is the creation of a system with built-in inefficiencies; the trade-off is built-in stability and responsiveness as well.

The same principles operate at the institutional level for those types that generalize rather than specialize. Whether this is done by building enough slack into the organizations so they can adapt to changing environments (thus making their ongoing operations less efficient) or by ensuring only loose coupling between specialized subunits (thus making institutions look improperly managed), the effect is the same: Generalized institutions have excess capacity that may appear wasteful but that in fact provides the means by which they can buffer environmental reverses that could destroy specialized schools.

Invariably, generalized institutions will have more excess capacity, or slack, than they really "need"; the problem is deciding a priori what is and what is not needed. There is no way to do this. "In a rapidly changing environment, the definition of excess capacity is likely to change frequently. What is used today may become excess tomorrow, and what is excess today may be crucial tomorrow. . . . Whereas those charged with assessing performance will be tempted to view such allocations as wasteful, they may be essential for survival" (Hannan and Freeman, 1977, p. 948).

As environmental resources decline over the next twenty years, increased concern for management efficiency and public accountability will most likely increase already strong tendencies (particularly in the public sector) to affect economies by eliminating "waste." At the state level, this may take the form of reducing the number of institutions, increasing the control of planning mechanisms to eliminate apparent duplication of effort, or discouraging the continuation of marginal institutions in the nonpublic sector. For individual campuses, concern for reducing cost may lead to adopting or imposing quantitative management techniques, discontinuing programs with declining enrollments, and attempting to couple more tightly subsystems through more structured and centralized decision making. These methods may increase adaption to present conditions, but they are likely also to limit future adaptability.

The natural selection perspective suggests the counterintuitive possibility that attempts to reduce waste may paradoxically increase it. In the words of the Carnegie Foundation (1976, p. 17), "We caution that the external search for small efficiencies and improvements in the short run may kill the spirit of initiative, the self-reliance, and the self-responsibility of higher education in the long run and thus, also, lead to major inefficiencies and to deterioration."

A preferable alternative is to move toward a system of accountability without increased controls, as proposed by the

Education Commission of the States (1980). Under such a system, in budget negotiations, public institutions would mutually agree to program objectives and proposed accomplishments. Institutions then would be free to manage themselves as they saw fit and be held accountable, through the budget, for outcomes rather than adherence to processes. This concept is consistent with the ecological requirement that diversity can be increased by reducing uniformity of constraints, and it should be seriously considered in those states whose present structures and regulations almost completely inhibit any real sense of campus autonomy.

Rational and Natural Selection: Planned and Unplanned Variation

Selection processes are essential to the development of systems that respond to changes within the environment. There are two fundamental types of selection: natural and rational. Although neither process operates in a "pure" form in most social (as opposed to biological) systems, populations of organizations can be selected by forces that generally fall on one side or the other of this gradient. It may be that over the past forty years, American higher education itself has moved rapidly from a point closer to the ideal natural selection process to one closer to the ideal rational selection process.

The process of natural selection was described in detail. In contrast, rational selection processes are deliberate and culturally self-conscious attempts by a social group to use knowledge of social processes and estimates of external factors as a substitute for natural selection in an "effort to think out in advance the relative adaptiveness of alternative cultural changes" (Campbell, 1969, p. 75). The cogitative and decision activities of rational selection are implemented in the higher education system through processes of planning. As Campbell pointed out, planning processes reduce the waste involved in natural selection. Rather than permitting a large number of naturalistic experiments to be tried and evaluated against environmental fitness, planning allows social systems to restrict the number of such experiments to those that appear to have the greatest chance of success. Eliminating large numbers of new organizations and structures with relatively low probability for survival presumably increases the system's efficiency.

Although rational selection appears to have become predominant in higher education systems, its ability to preserve diversity has significant constraints, chiefly the inherent limits to rationality. The amount and quality of available data concerning social systems in general and higher education systems in particular, paucity of knowledge about the interaction of present social and environmental conditions (much less future circumstances), and the difficulty of implementing planning decisions, even assuming that they can be made properly, all make rational planning exceptionally difficult.

Moreover, fitting institutions to niches relies upon a level of understanding of how niches are created and change that does not exist. Planners can envision only a small number of possible scenarios (most of them related to their previous limited experiences), and as a consequence, niches are most likely defined by the planners' needs, interests, and experiences (Boulding, 1981). The end result is that selection criteria become lodged in the decision makers rather than the environment (Weick, 1979).

Finally, planning processes tend to contribute to the increased centralization of the systems employing them, leading to greater commonality in values and norms, common definitions and structures, and still greater emphasis upon rationality. As a consequence, deviance is less likely, and as opportunities for deviance decrease, so does diversity.

Associated with the tension between natural and rational selection is the issue of planned versus unplanned variation. All models of change based upon selection require variation as an essential characteristic. Selection models are indifferent to the source of variation; planned variation results from strategy and choice, and unplanned variation results from change, error, and luck (Aldrich, 1979).

Although it is true that natural selection can occur in a system predominated by planned variation, it becomes increasingly unlikely as the system develops over time. One reason is that because of rational planning's tendency to be self-perpetuating and expanding, opportunities of error, chance, or luck are likely to be diminished and either unrecognized or "corrected" when they do occur. Another reason is that the limits to rationality make it impossible to *plan* the range and diversity of variety that potentially can exist. Planned variety is likely to develop the alternatives that look most similar to present ones.

Rational planning places a premium upon efficiency, and efficiency is likely to reduce or prevent innovation. "The finely tuned organization creates few novel variations in behavior because all its efforts are directed toward attaining current goals" (Zammuto, 1982, p. 155). Rational planning also requires the development of standardized procedures and systems for defining, collecting, analyzing, and distributing data. It is difficult to argue against making data available, but Trow (1975) commented that a "good deal of what has made great universities really creative has been a function of bad data collection" (p. 123). The reason for this contention is that the absence of data makes it possible for diverse practices to develop within various parts of institutions. If data for these practices were available, they would reveal inequalities that a rational system would be required to address and most likely to either reduce or eliminate.

Because of these limitations, to a great extent the concept of planned diversity is a contradiction in terms. Planning limits the alternatives considered and leads to consideration of fewer, not more, alternatives. These alternatives are unlikely to include the full range of possibilities and more likely to resemble existing structures and programs rather than innovative ones. And the nature of planning is that plans more likely reflect the values of the planners rather than the environment—lessons of the past rather than the needs of the future. Attempts to plan, to increase diversity by strengthening rational orientations and increasing centralization, ironically are likely instead to reduce it.

Rational planning is now integrated into the operations of many institutions, multicampus systems, and statewide higher education offices. Although waste and inefficiency are not problems in the biological world, with its vast resources, self-correcting subsystems, and infinite time, the same is not true for social systems. Diversity in social systems, although a critical value, is by no means the only one that must be considered, and attempting to prevent and/or correct high levels of slack in social systems (that is, minimize waste) is also important in a world of finite resources. An appropriate balance must be struck between efficiency and diversity so that neither is maximized but both are accommodated. To do so requires that planners and planning agencies undertake appropriate self-limitation, recognizing that encouraging unplanned variation and using natural selection processes, which protect the system and increase its responsiveness to the environment, are in their own vested self-interest. Planners can encourage diversity not by mandating new organizations or programs but by establishing constraint parameters within which institutions can function with relative autonomy, lifting systemic restraints to change, and exposing institutions to the environment's selection pressures.

One effective way of structuring planning so that it leads to these outcomes would be to move away from statewide coordinating boards and consolidating governing boards toward a system of statewide advisory councils, as recommended by the Carnegie Foundation (1976). The foundation suggested that although long-range planning is essential to the proper development of higher education, parties at interest or agencies with operating responsibilities cannot do so properly. Advisory council planning would not result in detailed regulation but would provide information and policy recommendations that would affect the decision-making process of budgetary authorities, institutions and systems, and students. One purpose of such a plan would be to "provide for diversity among institutions, which competition will not necessarily assure and may even tend to eliminate . . ." (p. 13). Such a change in state planning structure may appear drastic, but in the absence of evidence that state planning in the past has decreased costs or increased quality, there appears to be no compelling reason to continue it in its present form.

Protecting the Independent Sector

Many consider the strength and vitality of the nonpublic sector an essential hallmark of diversity in this country. The closing of institutions, predictions of mass institutional failures, and the anguished cries of college presidents faced with difficult budgetary situations have helped create the impression of the imminent demise of nonpublic higher education. This study's data suggest that the nonpublic sector is still strong and that claims of its demise are incorrect. The number of institutions in this sector has grown over twenty years, although not at the same rate as public institutions. Some nonpublic institutions have failed, but there is no reason to believe that the failure rate is much different than it traditionally has been.

Previous studies in the early 1970s, which announced to considerable fanfare that the nonpublic sector was in desperate financial straits, were followed later by less publicized research (Carnegie Council, 1977; Minter and Bowen, 1980a), which suggested that the problems foreseen had been largely avoided or corrected. A history of crying wolf, together with this study's data indicating the increased size of the nonpublic population, might suggest that there is no cause for future concern or a need to take any measures to ensure the maintenance of diversity the independent sector provides. Such conclusions are premature.

The ecological environment of the next twenty years promises to be significantly different from that of the previous twenty. Declining resource bases will increase selective pressures upon the higher education population, and public sector institutions will be favored in this competition for many reasons. They more likely will be buffered because of their governmental protection and larger size and the advantages of generalization during a period of coarse-grained instability. The generalized portion of the nonpublic sector will be competing in niches in which public institutions will have a significant advantage because of their lower tuition. If present policies continue, by the year 2000, there should be numerically and proportionally fewer nonpublic institutions, and one consequence will be a further reduction in the system's diversity.

Diversity will be reduced because of the loss of institutions and the potential loss of institutional types. In 1980, 410 public institutions represented 46.3 percent of the study sample but only 30.4 percent of the institutional types. The nonpublic sector included 53.7 percent of the institutions in the sample but 69.6 percent of the institutional types. Because the nonpublic sector is therefore somewhat more diverse than the public one, the loss of, for example, 200 public institutions over the next twenty years would have less impact upon diversity than the loss of 200 nonpublic organizations.

Evidence suggests that in many ways the private sector is different than the public sector (see, for example, Carnegie Council, 1977; El-Khawas, 1976; Shulman, 1974; Jonsen, 1978). If it is in the public interest to maintain and indeed increase diversity, then it is also in their interest to ensure the vitality of the private sector.

If the marketplace were completely free, there would be no need to consider supporting one or another sector since natural selection would ensure its responsiveness to changing environmental needs. But the system is not a free market, and maintaining diversity during the next two decades is likely to require some specific public policy decisions. The arguments in support of the private sector (see, for example, Benezet, 1976) are strong, and they become even more compelling if environmental vulnerability increases for one sector but not the other. As long as the marketplace is not free, steps will be required to control the tuition differentials that even now, but increasingly in the future, apply negative selection pressures upon nonpublic institutions.

It was pointed out that a more evenhanded approach to state support of public and private higher education basically involves choosing between two alternatives: taking steps to make public institutions more like private ones or initiating policies to make private institutions more like public ones (Breneman and Finn, 1978). Within these two general directions, a number of alternatives are possible (see, for example, Breneman and Finn, 1978; Carnegie Council, 1977).

Private institutions can be made more like public ones by

providing direct state support on a per capita or similar formula basis; by entering into contractual arrangements to provide specific services; or by providing their students with tuition subsidies either directly or through need-based scholarship programs, which therefore funnel disproportionate resources of the program into private institutions.

Public institutions can be made more like private ones by increasing their tuition levels (most such plans also increase student aid availability), decreasing public subsidies, or issuing vouchers. The various social and political aspects of vouchers, however, for all practical purposes would appear to prevent their implementation.

Within these two basic policy directions are a myriad of possible alternatives and variations. The optimal program has not yet been invented, and it may have to be discovered through processes of political natural selection itself, but most likely it would have certain characteristics. It would provide a level of support high enough to prevent tuition differentials unrelated to program costs from being the primary factor in institutional survival. On the other hand, it would not provide support levels so high that institutions were protected from desirable environmental pressure. It would have as few controls as possible, to prevent the independent sector from becoming quasi-public and therefore losing the very characteristics that make its survival so important (Carnegie Foundation, 1976).

The most effective response is to encourage fair competition in the student marketplace (Carnegie Council, 1980). From the perspective of diversity, fair competition does not require that the price be the same for students at public and private institutions. In general, the average cost of private higher education is greater than at comparable public institutions, and for many students its perceived quality is also greater. There are few reasons why students should not be expected to pay a premium to attend a nonpublic college, and many students are willing to do so. However, as the price differential between public and private campuses increases, even students who would prefer to attend a private college increasingly become likely to enter the public sector (Tierney, 1982).

To a great extent, public institutions are buffered from the effects of competition because governments subsidize their costs and permit low prices as a matter of public policy. Continuing existing policies and providing future public budget appropriations on the same past basis is likely to increase still further the price differentials between public and private colleges. This will further increase private schools' vulnerability during an era of generally declining resources and most certainly will reduce diversity.

Of all the proposals made concerning this issue, the one that would seem to best protect diversity, at the same time supporting other important policy objectives, is the development of state programs of need-based grants, coupled with moderate increases in public institution tuition levels. Under such a plan, grants would be available to students attending either public or private colleges, and at least a portion of increased costs in public institutions would be supported by increased tuition charges rather than appropriations. To further increase variability, instead of all public institutions charging a uniform tuition, those in a state system might be given a range of tuition levels within which they could be permitted to decide what their school should charge. It would then be possible for institutions to develop new programs and approaches even if they were costly—and at the same time to expose themselves to selection processes if their decision later led them to greater or lesser fitness within the environment.

The support level of the need-based grants program could be adjusted so that it would either maintain in the future public-private tuition differentials in states that presently considered them acceptable or moderately decrease them over time in states that presently considered them too high. All such changes, including the initial implementation, should be made over an extended period of at least five years to avoid the possible massive and unanticipated consequences that often accompany significant interventions into complex and little-understood ecological systems.

This policy change would reflect a market-economy approach that would strengthen diversity. Decisions concerning institutions' birth, death, and transformation then would be much more subject to the environmental demands represented by the choices of numerous consumers rather than by the presumably rational, but inherently limited, views of state agencies and governing boards.

This form of student aid would be of greatest value to lower-income students, whose attendance decisions are particularly sensitive to price and whose opportunities to attend private institutions are reduced as price differentials increase. The need-based elements of such a program would ensure no reduction in access for such students despite the moderate increases in tuition in the public sector.

Finally, this type of funding mechanism would avoid several problems of institutional entitlement programs, such as those experienced in New York State. Under that state's Bundy Program, to qualify for assistance that for some meant the difference between failure and at least temporary survival, a number of institutions not only changed their control from religious to independent but altered their missions and curricula. This is a perfect example of the unanticipated consequences of interventions into complex social systems, for although many institutions survived, the changes they were required to make made them more, rather than less, like each other. Rather than increase diversity, programs providing direct support to independent institutions may reduce it.

Providing portable resources to students rather than institutions also avoids potential church-state entanglements and can benefit religious, independent, and proprietary institutions alike. It would not only maintain or perhaps even increase diversity, but it would do so while avoiding the state's disruptive and intrusive behavior.

The Future of Diversity

The maintenance and enhancement of diversity are critical to the future stability and responsiveness of the American system of higher education. Individual institutions can do certain things to increase (but by no means guarantee) their competitive position and make it more likely that colleges and universities of their type will be represented in the institutional population of the future.

Institutions in stable environments can:

- specialize rather than generalize
- control growth and organizational complexity
- focus their recruiting efforts and emphasize retention programs
- coordinate or centralize governance
- reduce concern for planning and increase concern for prudent management
- maintain tight links with constituencies

Institutions in unstable, fine-grained environments can:

- specialize rather than generalize
- control growth and organizational complexity
- emphasize staffing flexibility
- emphasize planning
- use surpluses to improve quality and buffer future deficits

Institutions in unstable, coarse-grained environments can:

- generalize
- decentralize governance and management
- loosely couple their organizational subunits
- deemphasize long-range planning and emphasize strategic environmental surveillance
- expand generalized recruitment efforts
- pay particular attention to staffing flexibility, retraining, and alternatives to tenure outside the institutional core

Within certain limits, institutions may be able to affect their destinies. But in important ways, the future of the system is not tightly linked to the future of individual institutions, and facilitating the processes of natural selection transcends issues of institutional survival. This means that it is more important to establish policies that can enhance diversity throughout the system than to focus upon what institutions can do to become more competitive. Although federal programs, particularly those related to student assistance, will have some effect upon the future of diversity, the major influence in the foreseeable future will probably continue to be the individual states and their governing and coordinating boards.

State governing and coordinating boards could facilitate diversity by:

- relaxing rigid criteria for approval of new programs
- developing two levels of institutional approval, one signifying absence of fraud and one identifying compliance with minimum standards
- becoming more active in disseminating comparative institutional data to make the marketplace more knowledgeable
- granting fiscal and management autonomy to public institutions and holding them accountable for results, not processes
- reducing regulations establishing uniform environmental constraints
- refraining from "bailing out" individual institutions, public or private
- recognizing the need for slack, particularly in large, complex institutions
- permitting institutions to place appropriated funds saved through prudent management into reserves to be used in lean times
- decreasing public/nonpublic tuition differentials through need-based student financial aid programs and increased public institution tuitions

Providing some level of support to students in nonpublic institutions will be difficult politically during the next two decades. In particular, institutions in the public sector are likely to fight such action on the grounds that public funds should not be funneled to private institutions while at the same time support in the public sector is cut back. The arguments in this study, however, suggest that diversity is itself of such critical importance that its support is in the public interest and outweighs that claim. The survival of all institutional types is caught up in a large and complex ecological system in which the future of one segment depends to a large but unknown extent upon the future of the others. Simplifying the system by permitting sectors to fail while protecting others through special environmental buffering may ultimately be to the detriment of the entire population.

Appendix: Reconsidering the Model

The natural selection and resource dependence models both focus upon the relationship of organizations to the environment. The natural selection perspective considers the changes of populations of organizations in response to the availability of niches that are more fit for one species than another. A resource dependence view looks at the way individual organizations adapt to changing environments by either adjusting their tactics and strategies or actively changing the environment itself. This study's findings suggest that the natural selection model can explain some, but by no means all, of the dynamics of change within the higher education system.

There are at least four reasons why natural selection may not be as completely applicable to organizational units as to biological ones: the role of government, the problem of population segmentation, the differences between genetic and social change, and the strategic potential of organizations.

In general, organizations that are part of governmental structures at the local, state, or national level or that in some other way come under the protection of governmental bodies have lower failure rates than do other organizations (Hannan and Freeman, 1977; Aldrich, 1979; Aldrich and Pfeffer, 1976). This protection partially buffers certain institutions from the environment and therefore, to some extent, reduces selection pressures. State protection occurs because it embeds institutions within a larger bureaucratic structure with high inertia, and the various political pressures that led to the establishment of specific public institutions in the first instance also prevent their demise. The inability of the University of Wisconsin system in the mid-1970s to close a small, cost-ineffective, two-year campus because the legislature refused to permit doing so suggests the advantages of an institution being publicly controlled. Such "anti-eugenic actions of the state" (Hannan and Freeman, 1977, p. 960) obviously diminish the natural selection model's applicability. Such actions do not eliminate it, however. This study's data suggest that public institutions are not as completely protected from failure as has been commonly assumed. Although it is true that a large proportion of the failed public institutions in the sample resulted from a policy decision in one state (ironically, Wisconsin) to eliminate its normal schools, other public institutions have been closed or merged as well. A decrease in the level of protection previously afforded publicly sponsored educational organizations has already begun in the lower schools. As the number of students enrolled in public elementary and secondary schools diminishes, cost-conscious school boards are closing many of these institutions. There is speculation that public colleges will soon fall under the same pressures and that fiscal crises at the state level will overcome previous reluctance to close public colleges. There is already evidence that large numbers of public institutions are "losing ground" financially (Minter and Bowen, 1980b) compared to institutions in the private sector! Even if this does not occur, however, it has been argued that governmental support of institutions does not eliminate selective pressures but just moves them to a higher level. The consequence would be that rather than institutions failing, entire systems or networks could fail (Hannan and Freeman, 1977, p. 961).

A second factor limiting the applicability of the natural selection model to organizations is the effect of size upon survival. Studies of business organizations indicate that population is segmented and that large organizations are much less likely to fail than small ones (Aldrich and Pfeffer, 1976; Aldrich, 1979). Larger organizations' relatively large resource base appears to buffer them against environmental changes that present strong selective pressures to smaller ones. This study's data indicate that this segmentation occurs in colleges and universities as well; large institutions never fail, and small ones often do. It appears that the natural selection model is thus more useful for studying small rather than larger institutions, and selection processes appear more probable in one subpopulation than in the other.

A third problem in applying natural selection to organizations is the differences between change processes in biological and social systems. Evolution in biological systems operates as genetic variations are positively or negatively selected by their adaptation to new or changing niches. Successful adaptations are retained and transmitted in the gene pool of the organism. Social evolution, although following the same principles of environmental selection, is not guided by a genetic structure but by instructions contained in other social artifacts. The availability of plans, computers, and other mechanisms for storing and transmitting such instructions means that, unlike biological ones, organizational instructions can change very rapidly (Boulding, 1981). Social systems also provide opportunities for conscious and planned cooperation or competition between members—a form of interaction not seen in biological evolution. Among other things, the consciousness of human beings means that niches for organizations are created not just by environmental factors but by the planned activities of people. Organisms respond to niches; humans create them. Goals, intentions, dreams of the future, new technologies, and the ability of humans and their organizations to adapt through learning rather than genetic change all differentiate between biological and social evolution. These differences mean that evolution that occurs over a large number of generations and an extended period of time in biological systems can take place over a short period in a social system. Data presented in preceding chapters show the significant changes in the distribution of organizational types over only twenty years.

Finally, individual organizations are able to change form

and structure to adapt to some changes in their environment, and in some cases, to change the environment itself—something no biological system can do. As discussed earlier, although most institutions' ability to engage in strategic choice is severely limited (Aldrich, 1979), this does not mean that it is proscribed. Data in Chapters Five and Six indicate that in only a twenty-year period, many changes in variables such as size, program, control, sex of a student body, ethnic composition, and degree level have been made by one or more institutions in the sample. Many of these changes resulted from conscious decision processes of the institution itself. During the last two decades, at least, *some* level of strategic choice was available to *some* institutions—an alternative that has no biological analogue. Changes of this nature blur the differences between the resource dependence and natural selection models since the outcomes of extreme adaptation and selection may be indistinguishable.

Considering these differences between biological and social systems leads to significant questions about the validity of natural selection as the sole mechanism for explaining changes in institutional populations. There is general agreement that organizations change in response to environmental pressures. But, as Hannan and Freeman (1977) pointed out, it is no more or less plausible to believe that one-to-one correspondence between environmental resources and social organization arises "from purposeful adaptation of organizations to the common constraints they face or because nonisomorphic organizations are selected against. Surely both processes are at work in most social systems" (p. 957).

At this stage in the development of organization theory, there is no definitive assessment of whether the natural selection or the resource dependence model offers the most useful approach to studying changes in organizational systems. The natural selection orientation is itself new and has not been subject to intensive empirical analysis. It is likely that both models have value, resource dependence for studying changes in individual institutions over relatively short periods, and natural selection for considering changes in populations of institutions over longer periods.

Perhaps the two approaches will be combined eventually. Aldrich and Pfeffer (1976), for example, discussed the use of the natural selection model to account for changes in organizational structure and activities of subunits that do not lead to elimination of the entire organization. In a way, this appears to treat at least some aspects of strategic choice and resource acquisition as factors that can be environmentally selected. This idea is based upon the unique ability of social but not biological organisms to modify part of their structure. Aldrich and Pfeffer (p. 85) wrote:

> Modifying the natural selection model in this fashion complicates an ecological analysis, since the criterion for successful adaptation to the environment is changed from the easier-to-observe survival or failure to the more problematic criterion of structural change or stability. Rather than being able to observe a population of organizations adapting by the selective elimination of the less fit, we may find that almost all survive, but that each has undergone significant internal transformations of structure. Nevertheless, modifying the ecological model is a necessary step toward recognizing the difference between organic and social evolution, and toward making natural selection theory useful for organizational analysis.

The usefulness of both models for studying higher education probably will be made more clear by examining data collected during the next twenty years, rather than that of the last twenty, since the availability of resources will decline and environmental pressures consequently will increase. In the meantime, this study focused upon natural selection to begin to redress the balance toward resource dependence, which has previously characterized the study of colleges and universities as organizations.

References

Aldrich, H. E. *Organizations and Environments.* Englewood Cliffs, N.J.: Prentice-Hall, 1979.

Aldrich, H. E., and Pfeffer, J. "Environments of Organizations." *Annual Review of Sociology,* 1976, *2,* 79-105.

Altman, R. A. *The Upper Division College.* San Francisco: Jossey-Bass, 1970.

American Association of University Professors. *Policy Documents and Reports.* Washington, D.C.: American Association of University Professors, 1977.

American Junior Colleges. Washington, D.C.: American Council on Education, 1960.

American Universities and Colleges. (8th ed.) Washington, D.C.: American Council on Education, 1960.

Anderson, C. L. *Land-Grant Universities and Their Continuing Challenge.* East Lansing: Michigan State University Press, 1976.

Anderson, R. E. *Strategic Policy Changes at Private Colleges.* New York: Teachers College Press, 1977.

Astin, A. W. "An Empirical Characterization of Higher Education." *Journal of Educational Psychology,* 1962, *53* (5), 224-235.

Astin, A. W. *The College Environment.* Washington, D.C.: American Council on Education, 1968.

Astin, A. W. *Preventing Students from Dropping Out.* San Francisco: Jossey-Bass, 1975.

Astin, A. W. *Four Critical Years.* San Francisco: Jossey-Bass, 1977.

Astin, A. W., and Henson, J. W. "New Measures of College Selectivity." *Research in Higher Education,* 1977, *6,* 1–9.

Astin, A. W., and Holland, J. "The Environmental Assessment Technique: A Way to Measure College Environments." *Journal of Educational Psychology,* 1961, *52,* 308–316.

Astin, A. W., King, M. R., and Richardson, G. T. *The American College Freshman: National Norms for 1979.* Los Angeles: Graduate School of Education, University of California, 1979.

Astin, A. W., and Lee, C. B. T. *The Invisible Colleges: A Profile of Small, Private Colleges with Limited Resources.* New York: McGraw-Hill, 1972.

Astin, A. W., and Solomon, L. C. "Measuring Academic Quality: An Interim Report." *Change,* 1979, *11,* 48–51.

Baird, L. L., Hartnett, R. T., and associates. *Understanding Student and Faculty Life.* San Francisco: Jossey-Bass, 1980.

Baldridge, J. V., and others. *Policy Making and Effective Leadership.* San Francisco: Jossey-Bass, 1978.

Barker, R. G., and Gump, P. V. *Big School, Small School.* Palo Alto, Calif.: Stanford University Press, 1964.

Barron's Profiles of American Colleges, Vol. 1: Descriptions of the Colleges. (12th ed.) New York: Barron's Educational Series, 1980.

Belitsky, A. H. *Private Vocational Schools: Their Emerging Role in Postsecondary Education.* Kalamazoo, Mich.: W. E. Upjohn Institute for Employment Research, 1970.

Bell, D. P. *A National Study of Upper-Level Institutions.* Washington, D.C.: American Association of State Colleges and Universities, 1981.

Ben-David, J. *American Higher Education: Directions Old and New.* New York: McGraw-Hill, 1972.

Benezet, L. T. *Private Higher Education and Public Funding.* Washington, D.C.: American Association for Higher Education, 1976.

Blackburn, R., and others. *Changing Practices in Undergraduate Education.* Berkeley, Calif.: Carnegie Council on Policy Studies in Higher Education, 1976.

Blau, P. M. *The Organization of Academic Work.* New York: Wiley, 1973.

Blau, P. M., and Margulies, R. Z. "The Reputations of American Professional Schools." *Change,* Winter 1974–1975, *6,* 42–47.

Boulding, K. E. "In Praise of Inefficiency." *AGB Reports,* January/February 1978, pp. 44–48.

Boulding, K. E. *Evolutionary Economics.* Beverly Hills, Calif.: Sage, 1981.

Bowen, H. R. *Investment in Learning.* San Francisco: Jossey-Bass, 1977.

Bowen, H. R., and Minter, W. J. *Private Higher Education: First Annual Report on Financial and Educational Trends in the Private Sector of American Higher Education.* Washington, D.C.: Association of American Colleges, 1975.

Bowen, H. R., and Minter, W. J. *Private Higher Education: Second Annual Report on Financial and Educational Trends in the Private Sector of American Higher Education.* Washington, D.C.: Association of American Colleges, 1976.

Bowles, F., and DeCosta, F. A. *Between Two Worlds: A Profile of Negro Higher Education.* New York: McGraw-Hill, 1971.

Breneman, D. W., and Finn, C. E., Jr. *Public Policy and Private Higher Education.* Washington, D.C.: The Brookings Institution, 1978.

Breneman, D. W., and Nelson, S. C. *Financing Community Colleges: An Economic Perspective.* Washington, D.C.: The Brookings Institution, 1981.

Brick, M. *Forum and Focus for the Community College Movement.* New York: Teachers College Press, 1963.

Briggs, K. A. "The American Mission." *The New York Times Magazine,* Feb. 14, 1981, p. 29.

Brubacher, J. S., and Rudy, W. *Higher Education in Transition: A History of American Colleges and Universities, 1636–1976.* New York: Harper & Row, 1976.

Bruno, J. E. *Educational Policy Analysis.* New York: Crane, Russak & Company, 1976.

Cameron, K. "Measuring Organizational Effectiveness in Institutions of Higher Education." *Administrative Science Quarterly,* 1978, *23,* 604–632.

Campbell, D. T. "Variation and Selective Retention in Socio-Cultural Evolution." *General Systems: Yearbook of the Society for General Systems Research,* 1969, *16,* 69–85.

Campbell, D. T. "On the Conflicts Between Biological and Social Evolution and Between Psychology and Moral Tradition." *American Psychologist,* December 1975, 1103–1126.

Carnegie Commission on Higher Education. *Less Time, More Options.* New York: McGraw-Hill, 1971a.

Carnegie Commission on Higher Education. *New Students and New Places: Policies for the Future Growth and Development of American Higher Education.* New York: McGraw-Hill, 1971b.

Carnegie Commission on Higher Education. *A Classification of Institutions of Higher Education.* Berkeley, Calif.: Carnegie Commission on Higher Education, 1973a.

Carnegie Commission on Higher Education. *The Purposes and the Performance of Higher Education in the United States.* New York: McGraw-Hill, 1973b.

Carnegie Council on Policy Studies in Higher Education. *A Classification of Institutions of Higher Education.* (Rev. ed.) Berkeley, Calif.: Carnegie Council for the Advancement of Teaching, 1976.

Carnegie Council on Policy Studies in Higher Education. *The States and Private Higher Education.* San Francisco: Jossey-Bass, 1977.

Carnegie Council on Policy Studies in Higher Education. *Three Thousand Futures: The Next Twenty Years for Higher Education.* San Francisco: Jossey-Bass, 1980.

Carnegie Foundation for the Advancement of Teaching. *More*

than Survival: Prospects for Higher Education in a Period of Uncertainty. San Francisco: Jossey-Bass, 1975.

Carnegie Foundation for the Advancement of Teaching. *The States and Higher Education.* San Francisco: Jossey-Bass, 1976.

Cartter, A. M. *An Assessment of Quality in Graduate Education.* Washington, D.C.: American Council on Education, 1966.

Cartter, A. M., and Solomon, L. C. "The Cartter Report on the Leading Schools of Education, Law and Business." *Change,* 1977, *9,* 44–48.

Chickering, A. W. *Education and Identity*. San Francisco: Jossey-Bass, 1969.

Clark, B. R. *The Distinctive College.* Chicago: Aldine, 1970.

Clark, B. R. "The Benefits of Disorder." *Change,* October 1976, pp. 31–37.

Clark, B. R. "The Role of Distinctiveness in College Development." In H. B. Sagen, H. R. Bowen, and B. R. Clark, *Career Preparation in the Independent Liberal Arts College.* Chicago: Associated Colleges of the Midwest, 1978.

Clark, B. R. "The Insulated Americans: Five Lessons from Abroad." In P. G. Altbach and R. O. Berdahl (Eds.), *Higher Education in American Society*. Buffalo, N.Y.: Prometheus Books, 1981.

Clark, B. R., and Youn, T. I. K. *Academic Power in the United States*. Washington, D.C.: American Association for Higher Education, 1976.

The College Blue Book (Narrative Descriptions). (17th ed.) New York: Macmillan, 1979.

The College Blue Book (Tabular Data). (17th ed.) New York: Macmillan, 1979.

The College Handbook 1979–80. (17th ed.) New York: College Entrance Examination Board, 1979.

Cross, K. P. *Beyond the Open Door.* San Francisco: Jossey-Bass, 1976.

Cuninggim, M. "Varieties of Church-Relatedness in Higher Education." In R. R. Parsonage (Ed.), *Church-Related Higher Education.* Valley Forge, Pa.: Judson Press, 1978.

Dunham, E. A. *Colleges of the Forgotten Americans.* New York: McGraw-Hill, 1969.

Education Commission of the States. *Challenge: Coordination and Governance in the 80's.* Denver: Education Commission of the States, July 1980.

Ehrlich, P. R. "Diversity and the Steady State." Unpublished manuscript, Department of Biological Sciences, Stanford University, 1979.

El-Khawas, E. H. *Public and Private Higher Education Differences in Role, Character, and Clientele.* Washington, D.C.: American Council on Education, 1976.

Erickson, E. W., and others. *Proprietary Business Schools and Community Colleges: Resource Allocation, Student Needs, and Federal Policies.* Prepared for the Assistant Secretary for Planning and Evaluation, U.S. Department of Health, Education and Welfare, June 10, 1972.

Feldman, K. A., and Newcomb, T. M. *The Impact of College on Students.* San Francisco: Jossey-Bass, 1969.

Feldman, P. N. J. "Education Officials Put Heads Together." *The Sunday Record,* Nov. 22, 1981, sec. A, p. 14.

Finn, C. E., Jr. *Scholars, Dollars, and Bureaucrats.* Washington, D.C.: The Brookings Institution, 1978.

Freeman, R. B. *The Overeducated American.* New York: Academic Press, 1976.

Gaff, J. G. "Making a Difference: The Impacts of Faculty." *Journal of Higher Education,* November 1973, pp. 605-622.

Gappa, J. M., and Uehling, B. S. *Women in Academe: Steps to Greater Equality.* Washington, D.C.: American Association for Higher Education, 1979.

Gittell, M., and Dollar, B. "Cultural Pluralism: Traditional and Alternative Models in Higher Education." In A. Pantoja, B. Blourock, and J. Bowman (Eds.), *Badges and Indicia of Slavery: Cultural Pluralism Redefined.* Lincoln: University of Nebraska, 1975.

Grant, G., and Riesman, D. *The Perpetual Dream: Reform and Experiment in the American College.* Chicago: University of Chicago Press, 1978.

Greeley, A. M. *From Backwater to Mainstream: A Profile of Catholic Higher Education.* New York: McGraw-Hill, 1969.

Gross, E., and Grambsch, P. V. *University Goals and Academic Power.* Washington, D.C.: American Council on Education, 1968.

Gross, E., and Grambsch, P. V. *Changes in University Organization, 1964–71.* New York: McGraw-Hill, 1974.

Handlin, O., and Handlin, M. F. *The American College and American Culture: Socialization as a Function of Higher Education.* New York: McGraw-Hill, 1970.

Hannan, M. T., and Freeman, J. "The Population Ecology of Organizations." *American Journal of Sociology,* 1977, *82,* 929–964. © 1977 by The University of Chicago. All rights reserved. Portions reprinted by permission.

Harcleroad, F. F. "Private Constituencies and Their Impact on Higher Education." In P. G. Altbach and R. O. Berdahl (Eds.), *Higher Education in American Society.* Buffalo, N.Y.: Prometheus Books, 1981.

Harcleroad, F. F., Molen, T., Jr., and Van Ort, S. *The Regional State Colleges and Universities in the Middle 1970's.* Tucson: Higher Education Program, University of Arizona, 1976.

Hardin, G. J. *Nature and Man's Fate.* New York: Holt, Rinehart and Winston, 1959.

Hawley, A. H. "Human Ecology." In D. L. Sills (Ed.), *International Encyclopedia of the Social Sciences.* New York: Crowell Collier and Macmillan, 1968.

Hobbs, W. C., and Meeth, L. R. *Diversity Among Christian Colleges.* Arlington, Va.: Studies in Higher Education, 1980.

Hodgkinson, H. L. *Institutions in Transition.* New York: McGraw-Hill, 1971.

Jencks, C., and Riesman, D. *The Academic Revolution.* Chicago: University of Chicago Press, 1977. (Originally published 1968.)

Jonsen, R. W. *Small Liberal Arts Colleges: Diversity at the Crossroads?* Washington, D.C.: American Association for Higher Education, 1978.

Kaplan, M. (Ed.). *The Monday Morning Imagination.* New York: Aspen Institute for Humanistic Studies, 1976.

Kast, F. E., and Rosenzweig, J. E. *Contingency Views of Organ-*

ization and Management. Chicago: Science Research Associates, 1973.

Katz, D., and Kahn, R. L. *The Social Psychology of Organizations.* (2nd ed.) New York: Wiley, 1978.

Keeton, M. T. *Models and Mavericks: A Profile of Private Liberal Arts Colleges.* New York: McGraw-Hill, 1971.

Kemerer, F. R., Baldridge, J. V., and Green, K. C. *Strategies for Effective Enrollment Management.* Washington, D.C.: American Association of State Colleges and Universities, 1982.

Kerr, C. *The Uses of the University.* New York: Harper & Row, 1964.

Krebs, C. J. *Ecology: The Experimental Analysis of Distribution and Abundance.* New York: Harper & Row, 1972.

Kuh, G. D. *Indices of Quality in the Undergraduate Experience.* Washington, D.C.: American Association for Higher Education, 1981.

Ladd, E. C., Jr., and Lipset, S. M. *The Divided Academy: Professors and Politics.* New York: McGraw-Hill, 1975.

Lazersfeld, P. F., and Thielens, W., Jr. *The Academic Mind: Social Scientists in a Time of Crisis.* Glencoe, Ill.: Free Press of Glencoe, 1958.

Levins, R. *Evolution in Changing Environments: Some Theoretical Explorations.* Princeton, N.J.: Princeton University Press, 1968.

MacArthur, R. "The Theory of the Niche." In R. H. Whittaker and S. A. Levin (Eds.), *Niche: Theory and Application.* Stroudsburg, Pa.: Dowden, Hutchinson & Ross, 1975.

McGrath, E. J. *The Predominantly Negro Colleges and Universities in Transition.* New York: Teachers College Press, 1965.

Maeroff, G. I. "Yeshiva U., Once Almost Bankrupt, Eagerly Awaits Final Debt Payment." *The New York Times,* Nov. 15, 1981, p. 58.

Makowski, D., and Wulfsberg, R. M. *An Improved Taxonomy of Postsecondary Institutions.* Boulder, Colo.: National Center for Higher Education Management Systems, 1980.

Malcolm King Harlem College Extension. "Final Report on FIPSE Project." Unpublished report submitted to the Fund for the Improvement of Postsecondary Education, Washington, D.C., 1975.

Martin, W. B. *Conformity: Standards and Change in Higher Education.* San Francisco: Jossey-Bass, 1969.

Mayhew, L. B. *Surviving the Eighties.* San Francisco: Jossey-Bass, 1979.

Minter, W. J., and Bowen, H. R. *Independent Higher Education: Fifth Annual Report on Financial and Educational Trends in the Independent Sector of American Higher Education.* Washington, D.C.: National Institute of Independent Colleges and Universities, 1980a.

Minter, W. J., and Bowen, H. R. *Preserving America's Investment in Human Capital: A Study of Public Higher Education, 1980.* Washington, D.C.: American Association of State Colleges and Universities, 1980b.

Mortimer, K. P., and McConnell, T. R. *Sharing Authority Effectively.* San Francisco: Jossey-Bass, 1978.

National Center for Education Statistics. *Educational Colleges and Universities, 1978-9.* Washington, D.C.: U.S. Government Printing Office, 1979.

National Center for Education Statistics. *The Condition of Education, 1980 edition.* Washington, D.C.: U.S. Government Printing Office, 1980a.

National Center for Education Statistics. *Digest of Educational Statistics, 1981.* Washington, D.C.: U.S. Government Printing Office, 1980b.

National Center for Education Statistics. *Education Directory, Colleges and Universities 1979-1980.* Washington, D.C.: U.S. Government Printing Office, 1980c.

National Center for Education Statistics. *Digest of Educational Statistics.* Washington, D.C.: U.S. Government Printing Office, 1981a.

National Center for Education Statistics. *Education Directory, Colleges and Universities 1981-82.* Washington, D.C.: U.S. Government Printing Office, 1981b.

National Congress on Church-Related Colleges and Universities. *Church and College: A Vital Partnership.* Sherman, Tex.: Austin College, 1980.

Newman, F. *Report on Higher Education.* Washington, D.C.: U.S. Department of Health, Education and Welfare, 1971.

Pace, C. R. *College and University Environmental Scales: Tech-*

nical Manual. (2nd ed.) Princeton, N.J.: Educational Testing Service, 1969.

Pace, C. R. *Education and Evangelism: A Profile of Protestant Colleges.* New York: McGraw-Hill, 1972.

Pace, C. R. *The Demise of Diversity? A Comparative Profile of Eight Types of Institutions.* New York: McGraw-Hill, 1974.

Pace, C. R. *Measuring Outcomes of College: Fifty Years of Findings and Recommendations for the Future.* San Francisco: Jossey-Bass, 1979.

Pfeffer, J., and Salancik, G. R. *The External Control of Organizations: A Resource Dependence Perspective.* New York: Harper & Row, 1978.

Riesman, D. *Constraint and Variety in American Education.* Lincoln: University of Nebraska Press, 1956.

Riesman, D. "The Future of Diversity in a Time of Retrenchment." *Higher Education,* 1975, *4,* 461-482.

Riesman, D. *On Higher Education.* San Francisco: Jossey-Bass, 1981.

Riesman, D., Gusfield, J., and Gamson, Z. *Academic Values and Mass Education.* New York: McGraw-Hill, 1970.

Roose, K. D., and Andersen, C. J. *A Rating of Graduate Programs.* Washington, D.C.: American Council on Education, 1970.

Rudolph, F. *The American College and University.* New York: Knopf, 1962.

Rudolph, F. *Curriculum: A History of the American Undergraduate Course of Study Since 1636.* San Francisco: Jossey-Bass, 1977.

Scott, W. R. *Organizations: Rational, Natural and Open Systems.* Englewood Cliffs, N.J.: Prentice-Hall, 1981.

Sexson, J. A., and Harbeson, J. W. *The New American College.* New York: Harper & Row, 1946.

Shulman, C. H. *Private Colleges: Present Conditions and Future Prospects.* Washington, D.C.: American Association for Higher Education, 1974.

Sloan Commission on Government and Higher Education. *A Program for Renewed Partnership.* Cambridge, Mass.: Ballinger, 1980.

Smart, J. C. "Diversity of Academic Organizations: Faculty Incentives." *Journal of Higher Education,* 1978, *49* (5), 403-419.

Smith, V. B., and Bernstein, A. R. *The Impersonal Campus.* San Francisco: Jossey-Bass, 1979.

Stadtman, V. A. *Academic Adaptations.* San Francisco: Jossey-Bass, 1980.

State Education Department. *New York State Bundy Aid Program, 1969-1979: A Historical Report on New York State Colleges and Universities Receiving State Aid Under Section 6401 of the Education Law.* Albany: State Education Department, 1979.

Tewksbury, D. G. *The Founding of American Colleges and Universities Before the Civil War.* New York: Teachers College, Columbia University, 1932.

Thompson, D. C. "Black College Faculty and Students: The Nature of Their Interaction." In C. V. Willie and R. R. Edmonds (Eds.), *Black Colleges in America: Challenge, Development, Survival.* New York: Teachers College Press, 1978.

Tierney, M. L. "The Impact of Institutional Net Price on Student Demand for Higher Education." *Economics of Education Review,* 1982, *2,* 363-383.

Trivett, D. A. *Proprietary Schools and Postsecondary Education.* Washington, D.C.: American Association for Higher Education, 1974.

Trow, M. "Student Cultures and Administrative Action." In R. L. S. Sutherland and others (Eds.), *Personality Factors on the College Campus.* Austin, Tex.: Hogg Foundation for Mental Health, 1962.

Trow, M. "The Public and Private Lives of Higher Education." *Daedalus,* 1975, *104* (1), 113-127.

Trow, M. "Aspects of Diversity in American Higher Education." In H. J. Gans and others (Eds.), *On the Making of Americans: Essays in Honor of David Reisman.* Philadelphia: University of Pennsylvania Press, 1979.

"Undergraduate Enrollment by Race in U.S. Colleges and Universities." *Chronicle of Higher Education,* February 2, 1981, *21* (21), 7-14.

U.S. Department of Health, Education and Welfare. *Education Directory, 1959–1960, Part 3, Higher Education.* Washington, D.C.: U.S. Government Printing Office, 1960.

U.S. Department of Health, Education and Welfare. *Education Directory, 1966–1967, Part 3, Higher Education.* Washington, D.C.: U.S. Government Printing Office, 1967.

Warren, J. R. *Report on Academic Competencies Project.* Berkeley, Calif.: Educational Testing Service, 1977.

Weick, K. E. "Educational Organizations as Loosely Coupled Systems." *Administrative Science Quarterly,* 1976, *21,* 1–18.

Weick, K. E. *The Social Psychology of Organizing.* (2nd ed.) Reading, Mass.: Addison-Wesley, 1979.

Whittaker, R. H. "Communities and Ecosystems." In R. H. Whittaker and S. A. Levin (Eds.), *Niche: Theory and Application.* Stroudsburg, Pa.: Dowden, Hutchinson & Ross, 1975.

Whittaker, R. H., and Levin, S. A. (Eds.). *Niche: Theory and Application.* Stroudsburg, Pa.: Dowden, Hutchinson & Ross, 1975.

Whittaker, R. H., Levin, S. A., and Root, R. B. "Niche, Habitat, and Ecotope." In R. H. Whittaker and S. A. Levin (Eds.), *Niche: Theory and Application.* Stroudsburg, Pa.: Dowden, Hutchinson & Ross, 1975.

Wildavsky, A. *Speaking Truth to Power: The Art and Craft of Policy Analysis.* Boston: Little, Brown, 1979.

Willie, C. V., and Edmonds, R. R. (Eds.). *Black Colleges in America: Challenge, Development, Survival.* New York: Teachers College Press, 1978.

Worthington, R. M. "Career Education: An Alliance with Private Vocational Schools." Address to National Association of Trade and Technical Schools, 8th annual conference, Washington, D.C., June 1972. Reported in *Congressional Record,* H.R., vol. 119, Jan. 6, 1973.

Zammuto, R. F. *Assessing Organizational Effectiveness.* Albany: State University of New York Press, 1982.

Zammuto, R. F. Personal correspondence, Feb. 8, 1983a.

Zammuto, R. F. "Are Liberal Arts Colleges an Endangered Species?" Boulder, Colo.: National Center for Higher Education Management Systems, 1983b.

Index

O

P

Q

R

DATE DUE
May 24, 1994
MAR 19 1996
SEP 01 2008
GAYLORD